LEADER'S GUIDE   SPIRITUAL *Discovery* SERIES

Biblical Foundations

PRINCIPLES FOR THE PENTECOSTAL BELIEVER

DONALD F. JOHNS

Radiant Life
1445 N. Boonville Avenue
Springfield, MO 65802-1894
02-0218

PHOTO CREDITS:

©1997 Image Farm, Inc.: Cover, back cover; ©1997 PhotoDisc, Inc.: pp. 1, 3, 4, 5, 6, 7, 37, 58, 65, 73;
© 2002 PhotoSpin: pp. 9, 16, 31, 66, 94; Ricky Davis: p. 43; Karen Hollsinger Mullen: p. 24;
Rockefellow Studios: p. 51; Jim Whitmer: p. 88.

Fourth Printing 2014

©1997 by the Gospel Publishing House
Springfield, Missouri 65802-1894
Adapted from *Fundamentals Of The Faith* by Donald F. Johns

ISBN 978-0-88243-218-2
Printed in the United States of America

A Study Guide for individual or group study with this book is available
(order #02-0118).

Contents

WELCOME TO THE
SPIRITUAL *Discovery* SERIES

The *Spiritual Discovery Series* is a unique curricula product. It has been designed with today's learner in mind. A quick survey of this guide will reveal many changes from earlier texts. These changes reflect our philosophy of adult education. It is important that you, the teacher/facilitator, understand the reason for the changes and the educational philosophy used to develop the *Spiritual Discovery Series.*

First, you will note interactive questions strategically placed throughout the study guide material. Research reveals that adults want to participate in the process of learning. Too often Sunday School has become a place where students come to hear what the teacher has discovered that week. The *Spiritual Discovery Series* requires individuals to study the Scriptures and make personal discoveries. Not everyone has access to a theological library. With this in mind, our curriculum provides "hard to get" information while leaving the majority of work for the learner.

Second, you will note the only difference between the study guide and the leader's text is the suggested learning methodology. Some may wonder why no additional commentary is provided for the leader. The *Spiritual Discovery Series* places the teacher in the role of facilitator rather than class expert. The teacher/facilitator is seen as a partner in the learning process. The teacher/facilitator should complete the study guide and be prepared to bring his/her personal discoveries to the session to be added to the mix. The facilitator's primary function is to keep the group on track and moving. Activities (with approximate time to accomplish them) are provided to reinforce principles and move the group from point to point.

Third, you will note the *Spiritual Discovery Series*' writers do not tell learners how to live, but rather point them toward the only Book that has the authority to demand lifestyle reform. Our curriculum is merely a tool leading individuals to the Bible which alone contains definitive answers to life's problems.

The *Spiritual Discovery Series* is an excellent tool for those who wish to engage the minds of their fellow learners. You may feel uncomfortable with the change, but in a very short time you will be encouraged by the participation and the level of learning occurring among members of your group.

As always, we at *Radiant Life* welcome your comments. An evaluation form has been included in this guide. We encourage you to use it. It is our desire to continually improve our products to better meet the needs of those we serve. Thank you for using the *Spiritual Discovery Series*.

USING THE SPIRITUAL DISCOVERY SERIES LEADER'S GUIDE

1 **Study the objective before beginning each session.** It is important that you know what you wish to accomplish before you begin.

2 Read through the section entitled "What You Will Need" early enough in the week to **allow time to secure items necessary to direct the session efficiently.** Almost everything you will need to conduct a successful session is provided in the curriculum. Occasionally you will need to provide common items for illustrations. When these are needed, they will be clearly outlined in the "What You Will Need" section.

3 "Getting The Group's Attention" is one of the more important parts of the methodology. The leader must **grab the attention of the group from the very beginning.** Be sure to carefully plan this section of the session.

4 A transition statement is provided in each study to assist in the logical transition from "Getting The Group's Attention" to the main body of the study. **Reading the transition statement to the group will clearly define the study objective for everyone.**

5 **An overhead projector is a valuable communication tool** which is referred to throughout this study. If you do not have access to an overhead projector, write the information on a marker board or provide a copy of the overhead master for each group member.

6 The methodology used in this study includes discussion, short lectures, study guide responses, prayer, handouts, and brief presentations. Times have been approximated for each method. As the leader, you may **choose to use all of the suggested methods or select those most useful to you.**

7 **Provide opportunity for group members to apply principles** discovered in the session.

8 Encourage after-session fellowship.

GENERAL SUGGESTIONS TO THE GROUP LEADER

1 When leading a study group, the leader must **remember the Bible provides the answers and is the authority.** The leader facilitates discovery of biblical truths by the group. Always come prepared to contribute to the discovery process by completing the study guide material beforehand.

2 **Begin each session with prayer.** Invite the Holy Spirit to be your guide as you facilitate the discussion.

3 **Start on time and finish on time.** Starting late will reinforce tardiness. Finishing late will frustrate those who have made other plans and need to leave. Respect people's time.

4 The task of the leader/facilitator is to **keep the group moving and on target.** Avoid tangents. On occasion, the leader may choose to focus large amounts of group time on a particular point of interest, but this should be the exception. The good of the group should not be regularly sacrificed for the individual.

5 **Do not allow anyone to dominate the discussion, including yourself.** Encourage participation from those who seldom speak. The group benefits proportionately to the number who participate.

6 **Avoid restating or rewording people's answers.** If you think a response is not complete, or not clear to the group, you may wish to ask the group if they have anything to add to the last response.

7 **Never put a person on the spot** by asking him to read or pray aloud, without prior arrangement. Ask for volunteers rather than calling on a specific person.

8 In most cases, a variety of Bible translations will be present in the group. **Encourage readings from differing translations** to broaden the group's understanding of the text.

9 All the study questions are important. However, not all questions will demand an equal amount of group discussion time. Studies have been designed to be completed in 45 to 60 minutes. **Prioritize your time by determining an approximate amount of time to be spent on each activity in advance.**

STUDY 1

ALL HAVE SINNED

Society has made self-improvement very popular. It's almost impossible to keep track of all the new exercise equipment, beauty techniques, and fashions available to enhance one's appearance. But even those with no Bible knowledge realize that fixing up the exterior does not meet the underlying need they have in their lives. People try to ignore this deeper problem by busying themselves with self-improvement. What they don't realize is that ignorance is not always bliss.

God states untiringly that mankind's problem is that we have all fallen short of His requirements for us. All have sinned. No individual can escape this fact. In every race, economic level, age level, and career path, sin can be found. Only Jesus is sinless. This sin separates us from God, and in doing so, creates a feeling of emptiness. What we need to know is: What is sin and how does it affect our lives?

Only the death of Jesus could separate us from our state of sinfulness.

Study Objective

To acknowledge that all are sinners and accept the substitutionary death of Christ as hope for eternal life.

What You Will Need

☐ Enough copies of resource 1A, "What Do You Believe?" for each group member.
☐ An overhead projector and markers.
☐ An overhead transparency of resource 1B, "Agree/Disagree."
☐ Refreshments for the "Group Fellowship" time at the end of the session.

Getting The Group's Attention

(All times are estimates. 10 minutes)

Distribute a copy of resource 1A, "What Do You Believe?" to each individual. Give them 7 minutes to write out their responses. Then have several group members volunteer to share their responses to items 2 and 6. Allow for "friendly" discussion.

Have someone gather all the work sheets. You may be able to use these to assist you in preparation for upcoming sessions.

Transition Statement

THE IMPARTIAL STANDARD

Role Play
(10 minutes)

Have three individuals volunteer to role-play a job interview. One person will be the employer—a graduate of Smith High School. One person will be an applicant from Jones High School, and the other, a less qualified applicant also from Smith High School. Have them go through two brief interviews and let the Smith High School graduate get the job solely because of the school association.

Have group members discuss how they feel about the standard used for the selection process.

Ask the following questions:

1. "How would you feel about a god who helped you based on its current mood or what you've done for it lately?"

2. "How does an impartial standard for acceptance and salvation affect your attitude toward that salvation and the god providing it?"

God has held up the same standard of judgment to all people of all times—obedience to Him. This obedience is demonstrated in the life of every person who accepts salvation through Jesus Christ as the restoration of fellowship with God. What brings people to this point of restoration is the realization of their spiritual condition and the willingness to accept God's plan.

1. Read Isaiah 64:6 and Romans 3:23. What do these verses state about our spiritual condition?

_____

_____

_____

God requires obedience today just as He required obedience from Adam before the creation of Eve. Disobedience is sin.

2. In Genesis 2:16,17 what command did God give Adam and expect him to obey?

_____

_____

Even Eve was aware of God's command to Adam. In Genesis 3:3 when being tempted, she spoke it to Satan. She knew God had spoken to Adam, placing them under the obligation of obedience.

Later, God indicated that He expected obedience from the nation of Israel as He was delivering them from the bondage of Egypt. Israel was to be God's chosen people, but He nevertheless expected obedience from the nation.

3. Read Exodus 19:5,6; Deuteronomy 26:18; 28:1,9; 32:46,47. Record below the different times God expressed His desire for obedience from the Israelites in these passages.

_____

_____

_____

What would be the result? _____

_____

Twice Moses was called to the top of Mount Sinai by the Lord. The first time God spoke the Ten Commandments to Moses (Exodus 19:16 to 20:17). The second time, after 40 days and nights on the mountain, Moses retraced his steps down the mountain carrying with him the two tablets of stone (Exodus 24:12-18; 31:18). The Ten Commandments were the Law which God gave to His chosen nation to obey.

4. Read Romans 3:1,2; 9:4,5. What privileges given to Israel called for their obedience to God's Law?

_____

_____

_____

_____

✎ **5. According to Deuteronomy 28:9,10, why was Israel to obey God's laws?**

_____

_____

Israel was chosen and privileged, but obedience was still required of her. The Israelites were not exempt from obedience just because they were the chosen people.

God also requires the non-Jewish people of the world, biblically known as the Gentiles, to obey Him. They, as well as the Jews, are judged by God according to His impartial standard of obedience.

✎ **6. What do Acts 10:34,35 and Romans 2:11 reveal about God's expectation of obedience from people?**

_____

_____

_____

How can God expect obedience from the Gentiles if He has not given them the Law to obey? He does not hold the Gentiles responsible for sinning against the Law of the Old Testament. However, He does hold them responsible for sinning against the law which He has written in their hearts, and especially for their lack of response to the urging of the Holy Spirit to repent and accept Christ as their Redeemer.

God has given to all people, everywhere, a means of knowing right from wrong. The Law, as transmitted to Israel, enabled the Israelites to know right from wrong in an absolute and final way. Human experience does not give an absolute and final knowledge of right and wrong, but it does provide a relatively accurate knowledge of what is right and what is wrong. Failure to do what they know is right is to sin against God.

✎ **7. Read Romans 2:14,15. According to this passage what is expected of those who do not have the Law?**

_____

_____

_____

THE IMPARTIAL JUDGE

God does not show favoritism (Romans 2:11). He is an impartial Judge using the same standard for all people.

✎ **8. According to Romans 2:12,13, how can someone escape the judgment of God?**

_____

_____

_____

Every individual has received knowledge of what God wants him or her to do. Adam and Eve received this knowledge verbally. The Israelites received it in written form. The Gentiles discovered the rules of what is right and wrong as they experienced life. Each circumstance demonstrated what was the proper thing to do. The fairness of God caused Him to let every person receive knowledge. He then holds each person responsible for the knowledge they have and judges each one according to that knowledge.

▨ **Response**
(5 minutes)
Have group members share their responses to study guide items 6 and 7.

▨ **Brainstorm**
(3 minutes)
Ask, "Based on the information presented in the parallel column about how God gives each person a means of knowing right from wrong, why do we try to blame our sins on other people?"

Have individuals brainstorm whom or what they have tried to blame for their sins; e.g., Satan, society, family background, etc. Record their responses on an overhead transparency.

State: "Although we might try to place the blame for our sins on circumstances or other people, God makes it clear that each individual is responsible for his or her relationship of obedience to Him."

Guilty! God has made His verdict very clear. It holds true for all people. Adam and Eve disobeyed God by eating of the tree of the knowledge of good and evil.

9. Read Genesis 3:6. What motivated Eve and Adam to deliberately disobey God?

_____

_____

_____

Even though they were God's own creation, the Lord impartially judged Eve and Adam to be guilty because they had sinned against Him through disobedience.

10. Read Genesis 3:16-19. What were the specific judgments against Eve and Adam?

Eve _____

_____

_____

_____

Adam _____

_____

_____

_____

Adam and Eve suffered God's judgment and were banished from the Garden of Eden. Even today we still feel the effects of this verdict upon their disobedience.

When the nation of Israel received the Law through Moses, conditions were not greatly altered. Death had entered the world because of Adam and Eve's sin and had continued to the time of Moses.

11. Read Romans 5:12-14. What explanation for the continuation of death between the time of Adam and Moses can be found in this passage?

_____

_____

_____

12. Read Romans 3:19,20; 5:20. Did the Law eliminate the possibility of sin? Explain.

_____

_____

_____

_____

The sinful deeds of people did not cease when God gave the Law. The Law instead intensified the knowledge of sin. Yet theoretically, there is a possibility of attaining life through keeping the Law.

Discussion
(3 minutes)
Ask, "If God says we are all sinners, what keeps some people from admitting they are sinners?"

Have a few individuals share their responses to study guide item 9.

12

✎ **13. Read Leviticus 18:5 and Ezekiel 20:11. What do these verses say about what may be gained by keeping the Law?**

_____

_____

Compare the above Scripture references with Galatians 3:10 and James 2:10. What do these verses say about living by the Law?

_____

_____

_____

No one has ever kept the Law perfectly, so no one has ever attained life through Law-keeping (Galatians 3:11). The purpose of the Law was not to bring life. Its purpose was to place all under sin (Romans 2:12; 3:19; Galatians 3:23). Its purpose was to reveal guilt. God has rendered His impartial guilty verdict against the nation of Israel. Israel sinned under the Law and has been judged by the Law. Israel, God's chosen people, stands condemned before Him.

Although the Gentiles do not have the Law, they have learned that some things are right and others are wrong through the experiences of living. In the process of establishing this system of determining right and wrong, they have become a law unto themselves. Gentiles are responsible to live by the principles they have discovered. They have an obligation to live according to the highest and best that they know.

✎ **14. Read Romans 3:10,12. What verdict has been given by God to all people, including the Gentiles?**

_____

_____

Once again there is the impartial verdict. There are no exceptions to the sentence of God. Beginning with Adam and Eve, all mankind has sinned. Although only one sin is enough to brand the individual a sinner, people have indulged in repeated sinning. One sin is enough to condemn us, but none of us can point to only one mistake in our whole lifetime. All individuals who have ever lived or will live, except Jesus alone, are a part of the great company of sinners who have disobeyed God and come short of His glory.

What significance is there to the fact that all people have sinned through disobedience to God? There must be a reason for God to so explicitly demonstrate our sinfulness. There must be a penalty from which He wants to steer us.

✎ **15. Read Matthew 13:41,42; 25:46; Mark 9:43; Luke 16:19-31; John 5:28,29; 2 Thessalonians 1:9; and Revelation 20:15. How is the penalty for disobedience described in these passages?**

_____

_____

_____

_____

_____

_____

_____

✳ **Lecture**
(2 minutes)

Using the material from the parallel column, summarize the purpose of the Old Testament Law. You may wish to use responses from study guide items 11-14 to clarify.

✳ **Small Groups**
(5 minutes)

Divide the larger group into groups of three or four. Give the smaller groups 3 minutes to make a list of subtle sins people commit; e.g., gossip, gluttony, etc. Have the groups come back together and read aloud the following passages for Paul's lists of sins:

1 Corinthians 6:9,10
Galatians 5:19-21
Ephesians 4:25-31
Colossians 3:5-9

⇄ **Discussion**
(7 minutes)

Have group members discuss the following questions:

1. "What does the sinner have to look forward to at the final judgment and for eternity?"

2. "What should Christians be doing to help sinners escape such a judgment?"

3. "What can you do to help them?"

Response
(3 minutes)
Have group members share their responses to study guide item 16.

This doctrine is not always popular, but the Bible clearly teaches this truth. In today's society, when each person would like to be his or her own judge worshiping his or her own god, eternal punishment due to disobedience to the one true God is not palatable.

✎ **16. Read Romans 1:20-23. What does this passage say about the attitude of people about God throughout all time?**

_____

_____

_____

How have the events of Romans 1:24-32 been fulfilled in today's society?

_____

_____

_____

_____

In Matthew 10:28 Jesus warned His followers to fear the One who was able to destroy both soul and body in hell rather than one who could kill only the body here on earth. He intended that this truth of eternal punishment should change the behavior of the disciples. Eternal punishment is not just a scare tactic to get people to give up their sinful lives. It is an attempt to cause individuals to see the reality of their need for a relationship with God in which they obey His commands and not their own desires.

God has not left people without a solution upon the recognition of their need. He is not just an impartial Judge. He is also a loving, gracious Father. As much as He has pointed out the sinfulness of people, He has also revealed His plan for redemption from this eternal punishment.

✎ **17. Read 1 Timothy 2:4-6. What is God's desire for all people and how can this be accomplished?**

_____

_____

_____

_____

Overhead
(5 minutes)
Display resource 1B "Agree/Disagree" and uncover the statements one at a time. Give individuals time to express their opinions. Direct them to the appropriate answers as presented in this session and the Scripture passages provided on the overhead.

SUMMARY

All people throughout history have sinned against God. From Adam and Eve, to the giving of the Law, to the time of Jesus, to now—everyone has fallen short of God's standard. Jesus alone is sinless. As harsh a reality as it may seem, the punishment for this sinfulness is eternal torment in separation from God.

Nothing we can do can repair our relationship with God. Obedience is His expectation. But in ourselves, we are unable to fulfill this expectation. And sometimes in our efforts we only draw ourselves further away from Him.

But God, while demanding obedience impartially from all people and judging us all guilty, is loving and merciful. As our Creator, He desires that all people would come to know Him and be in relationship with Him. He has provided a way for us to reconcile ourselves to Him—Jesus Christ, His Son. By accepting His sacrifice as substitute for ours, we can be in right relationship with God and experience eternal life with Him.

LET'S REVIEW

✎ 1. If Israel was expected to obey God, in what way was Israel privileged?

_____

_____

_____

_____

✎ 2. How can God expect obedience from the Gentiles if He has not given them the Law to obey?

_____

_____

_____

_____

✎ 3. Does the Bible teach that life may be gained by keeping the Law? Explain.

_____

_____

_____

_____

_____

✎ 4. What is God's penalty for sin? What will be the future condition of sinners?

_____

_____

_____

_____

_____

✎ 5. What is God's desire for all people? How has He offered this opportunity?

_____

_____

_____

_____

_____

 Review
(3 minutes)

Select two or three study guide items from the "Let's Review" section to check the comprehension level of group members. If understanding of the study material seems weak, recommend that individuals work through the study again.

 Closing Prayer
(unlimited)

Ask if any in the group would like to make a salvation decision. If so, lead group members in a salvation prayer. If not, pray that God would continue to work in the hearts and lives of this group and show ways all can grow closer to Him.

Preparing For Next Session

Remind group members to complete study 2 before the next session.

Ask if anyone in the group would be willing to draw the New Jerusalem as described in Revelation 21:1 to 22:5 for the next session.

 Group Fellowship
(5 minutes)

Invite individuals to share in fellowship and refreshments before they leave.

Pass around a paper requesting group members to sign up to bring refreshments to the remaining sessions of the group study.

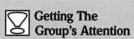

Study Objective

To consider the provision for reconciliation God has provided to all people and share His plan with those who have not heard it.

What You Will Need

☐ A copy of resources 2A, "The Lost Sons," and 2B, "Population Census," for each group member.
☐ A marker board or overhead projector and appropriate markers.
☐ A Bible word study tool, such as *Vine's Expository Dictionary Of Biblical Words*.

Getting The Group's Attention

(All times are estimates. 10 minutes)

Distribute a copy of resource 2A, "The Lost Sons," to each individual. Have group members gather into smaller groups of three or four. Give the groups 5 minutes to read Luke 15:11-32, and to observe how both brothers had distanced themselves from their father, not just the younger. Have them discuss the following question:

"How can we apply the story of the lost sons to our lives today?"

Have the larger group come together again and ask a representative from each smaller group to share some of his or her group's findings.

ALL CAN BE SAVED

The fact that everyone has sinned and is under the penalty of eternal punishment places a dark shadow over our lives. To live with this knowledge with no offering of hope would throw people into despair. Could a truly loving God leave us in this state of hopelessness?

God's resounding answer to that question is: No! Just like the sun breaking through after a dark storm, God presents His plan of hope to us—all can be saved. His desire is that no one would die in his or her sinful state, but would allow God to have His way in his or her heart. God's provision for individuals is not through church attendance or membership in a certain congregation. It is through belief on Jesus Christ and repentance of sins. It's really that simple and is impartially available.

Transition Statement ⇨ God has provided a means of reconciliation of himself to all people; we need only to repent and follow it.

NEEDED BY ALL

In God's sight, all people stand condemned and lost. It's all good and well to tell everyone they have sinned against God but some will ask, "In what way have I sinned?" God has identified the different ways people have sinned so that their sinfulness is stated more clearly.

 1. Read Psalms 5:9; 10:7; 140:3; Romans 3:13,14; and James 3:5,6,8. What descriptions of sinning are recorded in these passages?

_____

_____

_____

_____

Many people believe that this area of sinfulness is not serious. What are a few words of gossip, an angry remark under one's breath, a teasing comment taken the wrong way? Some people throw words around without thinking of their lasting effect on another individual. But God's Word makes it clear that He feels sins of this type are quite grievous. Reconsider the adjectives used in the above Scripture references. This instrument is violent and evil. None can tame it.

To sin by the use of hurting words would seem to include every person. If that doesn't impress an individual of his or her lack of perfection, there are other areas mentioned in the Bible.

 2. Read Isaiah 59:7 and Matthew 5:28; 15:18-20. What do these passages reveal as another source of sin in people's lives?

_____

_____

Why might this type of sin be so difficult to deal with? _____

_____

_____

_____

The person who sins in this fashion is just as guilty as the person who curses someone or slanders an acquaintance. Both need salvation. Behind the benign, smiling face of an individual can be hidden the vilest sins of the mind. Jesus makes it perfectly clear in Matthew 5:28 that according to God's standard to think of a crime is the same as committing the crime. And if thoughts are revealed in speech and actions, will they not be seen eventually anyway?

So, people sin in word and thought. There is one additional area in which individuals sin.

 3. Read Isaiah 59:6,7 and Romans 3:15,16; then read John 8:41,44. What realm of sin is identified in these references?

_____

Who is their source? _____

These acts are characteristic of people who need salvation. The person who has thought about a sin and talked about a sin is not far from following through with the acting out of that sin. The consequences of sin then reach out and touch other lives when the sin becomes expressed in an evil deed.

 Discussion
(6 minutes)

Have group members share their responses to study guide item 1. Ask a few volunteers to look up the passages listed and call out the adjectives used. Write these adjectives on a marker board or overhead transparency to stress the harm caused by this type of sin.

Now have individuals consider the childhood taunt, "Sticks and stones may break my bones but words will never hurt me."

Ask, "What degree of truth is contained in this statement? Explain."

Ask a volunteer to share a time when words hurt as much as a physical hit.

Response
(3 minutes)

Have a volunteer share his or her response to study guide item 2.

Usually those people who ask, "In what way have I sinned?" are speaking of outward acts of sin. Many of these persons may have hidden their sinful deeds from human view, but God sees everything that everyone does. He can read every thought, hear every word, and observe every deed. Who wants to be faced with a recording of all that he or she has thought, spoken, or done? Small wonder it can be said that every person has sinned and needs salvation.

PROVIDED FOR ALL

Just as God impartially judged all people of sin, so He impartially grants salvation to all who believe. God has provided it for everyone, but each individual must accept His gift of salvation.

 4. On the lines below, write out Romans 3:22-24 and memorize the passage.

_____

_____

_____

_____

_____

_____

_____

There are three theological terms that describe this salvation from God and its provision to restore a person's relationship with Him.

❏ *Justification.* God's salvation offers justification to the sinner. To be justified is to be accounted or declared righteous. When a person is justified or declared righteous, it does not mean that the person has never sinned. But the sinner does become, in God's sight, as though he had never sinned, declaring him or her to be righteous even though he or she has sinned. What a wonderful provision of salvation this is! God offers to forget the past, to wipe out the sins of people's lives, and to consider each one just and pure.

❏ *Propitiation.* God's salvation contains a propitiation. A propitiation is a satisfying atonement or appeasement which favorably alters a relationship. A person's sins bring him or her into an unfavorable relationship with God. This relationship has been positively adjusted through the payment Christ made on the cross for the sins of all people. Christ's shed blood is a propitiation for every person and satisfies the demands of God's righteousness and justice, atoning for sins. It enables God to call individuals just.

❏ *Redemption.* God's salvation provides complete redemption. *Redemption* means "buying back at a cost or a price."

 5. Read 1 Peter 1:18,19. Identify the price by which our redemption was bought and by what we are not redeemed.

_____

_____

The redeemed individual is no longer in bondage to self, sin, and Satan. He or she is liberated and made free to worship and serve God.

This great salvation is further evidence of God's impartiality and justness.

Activity
(3 minutes)
Ask a few group members who memorized the passage in study guide item 4 to recite it. Try to have different Bible versions or translations represented.

Justification =
Jesst as IF I've NEVER sinned.

Propitiation=
Reconciliation with God

Redemption -
Paid In Full

Small Groups
(7 minutes)
Have the group divide into smaller groups of four or five. Give the groups 4 minutes to define the three theological terms in the parallel column in their own words in a way relevant to them. Then have a representative from each group share their definitions with the larger group.

Response
(3 minutes)
Have group members share their responses to study guide item 5. Ask a volunteer to lead the group in singing the chorus, "Oh, How I Love Jesus," or another chorus thanking Jesus for His sacrifice for our salvation.

✎ **6. Read Romans 3:25,26. In what two ways did God demonstrate justice to mankind?**

_____

_____

_____

_____

God provided for us—those who have lived, do live, and will live on this earth. The salvation which He provided is adequate for all the sins of all the sinners who have ever lived and ever will live. He even provided a way for people who desired salvation before Christ lived on earth. For by faith they looked to God who redeemed them through the sacrifice which in God's plan had been made since the foundation of the earth.

✎ **7. Read Romans 3:27-30. What do these verses disclose about God's plan for redeeming people to himself?**

_____

_____

What part does the individual play in this plan? _____

God's salvation has not lost its power by the passage of time. It is still all that is needed for an individual to face the temptations and failures of the future. A person needs only to receive God's gift to experience a restored relationship with God.

OFFERED TO ALL

God not only has provided salvation for all, but He also offers salvation to all. He impartially extends His gift of salvation to every individual.

✎ **8. Read Ezekiel 18:32 and 2 Peter 3:9. What is revealed about God?**

_____

_____

_____

✎ **9. Now read 2 Peter 3:4-6. How did this instance of intervention demonstrate the above characteristic as well as God's judgment?**

_____

_____

_____

Because some people do not immediately accept salvation, God must often wait patiently. His desire that none should perish is the reason He exercised tolerance in the case of sins committed before the coming of Christ, risking having His righteousness called into question. It took the death of Christ to declare or prove that God was righteous in choosing not to punish those sins as soon as they were committed. Christ's death proved that God is not only interested in maintaining His own righteousness, but is also interested in making others righteous. If He were merely looking for an excuse to throw people into hell, God could easily find many. But God patiently waits for people to realize their need so He can save them. God is long-suffering and merciful, as well as just.

Handout
(5 minutes)
Distribute a copy of resource 2B, "Population Census," to each individual. Give everyone 2 minutes to look over the information on the handout. Ask, "In what ways do sinners find out about God's offer?"

Have group members share how they could help in the process of telling people, nearby and faraway, about the gift of God's salvation. Have each individual think of someone he or she could tell about Jesus this week.

✎ 10. How do Jesus' words in Matthew 24:14 demonstrate God's desire for all to turn to Him?

_____

_____

_____

Testimonies
(4 minutes)
Ask a few group members to volunteer to share their pre-salvation impression of God and what had brought each of them to that conclusion.
Ask each, "How did you feel about God immediately following your salvation?"

Satan would like people to see God as cruel and demanding, unjustly throwing weak, helpless humans into eternal torment. He portrays God as finding joy in damning souls. So many people see Him as Someone who is just waiting for them to make a mistake so that He can "zap" them. But the Bible gives the true picture of a loving but just God who gains no joy from the death of sinners. He would rather they all come to know Him and turn away from the wicked things they do (Ezekiel 33:11).

There are several phases involved in receiving the salvation which God offers to all.

❐ *Repentance.* To accept God's offer of salvation, the sinner must repent of his or her sins. This is more than simply feeling bad because of sins.

✎ 11. Read Ezekiel 18:21-23. Write out the definition of true repentance as it is described in this passage. What is the result of this repentance?

_____

_____

_____

Because God desires that all be saved rather than perish, He has made provision for repentance. The meaning of the word which is translated "repentance" is "a change of mind." To receive the salvation which God has offered to all, the sinner must change his or her mind about sin. He or she must view sin as God sees it. When this happens, the individual turns away from sin. This is the first step.

❐ *Faith.* By faith the sinner receives salvation. The repentant sinner longs to be free of the bondage of sin; by faith he or she permits Christ to break the bonds.

✎ 12. Read John 20:31; Romans 5:1; Galatians 2:15,16; 3:26-28; and Ephesians 2:8. What do these passages tell us about faith and its relationship to salvation? Where is it from?

Response
(3 minutes)
Have individuals share their responses to study guide items 12 and 13.

_____

_____

_____

The gospel truth of salvation by faith is so simple that many people completely miss it. They attempt to earn salvation, but it cannot be earned. God's offer through faith in Christ is available to all and must only be accepted. A conscious act of faith by the sinner must occur, then that person must believe that Christ actually enters into his or her life, and thank God for salvation. Faith, or belief, and salvation are inseparably linked together. All people, Jews and Gentiles, receive salvation upon the basis of faith, not upon the basis of works. Here again the impartiality of God is demonstrated. All must be saved in the same way—through faith.

✎ 13. Read Romans 6:23. What benefit results from demonstrating faith in Jesus Christ?

_____

❏ *Regeneration.* When the sinner repents and turns to God in faith, God regenerates or gives the sinner a rebirth.

✎ **14. Read John 3:3-6. Describe the type of rebirth received upon regeneration by God.**

_____

_____

✎ **15. According to 2 Corinthians 5:17, how does Paul explain regeneration?**

_____

_____

The person who asks Christ to come into his or her heart quickly realizes that things are different. When Christ enters He brings new life. By means of this spiritual birth, the sinner becomes spiritually alive as a child of God. (See John 1:12,13.) The person who is born again is no longer a child of disobedience, a child of Satan, and a child of wrath. God no longer views new believers as guilty of sin, but justifies them or declares them to be righteous because they have accepted Christ as their Savior and their righteousness.

Just as God has no favorites whom He protects against judgment, so He has no favorites to whom He offers exclusive rights to be saved. All people can be saved. God wants everyone to repent, to believe, to be regenerated.

✎ **16. Read Romans 10:13. What guarantee does a sinner have when he or she repents and asks God for salvation?**

_____

_____

_____

Sin and salvation both reach beyond this life into eternity—one into eternal torment and one into heavenly bliss. Salvation provides many rewards here on earth also. Christians are free from the guilt and power of sin, no longer captive to the lusts and desires of the flesh. They are brought into fellowship with God, candidates for Holy Spirit baptism, and experience peace and contentment they never imagined possible before they were saved.

All of these blessings are enjoyed on earth, during this present life. But the final reward of a Christian is not on this earth.

✎ **17. Read 1 Thessalonians 4:17. What is the ultimate reward for a Christian?**

_____

_____

_____

There is something within every person which longs for heaven. There seems to be an instinctive desire for heaven implanted within the heart of an individual. Even people who have never seen the Bible or heard the gospel message have created an imaginary heaven. Other religions of the world tell of a heaven which is patterned after their own ideas. People long for a place after death where all is joy and happiness.

The Bible gives us God's account of what heaven actually is like. Surely this universal need for heaven is something God has placed within people to make individuals look beyond the troubles and temptations of this present world. While banished on the Isle of Patmos, John had a vision of the eternal land he was soon to enter. This vision gives us one of the most detailed descriptions of heaven in all of its magnificence.

 Discussion
(3 minutes)
Have group members share their responses to study guide item 17.
Ask, "What do you feel is the greatest reward for a Christian (you) while still here on earth?" Have a few individuals explain their responses.
Follow up with, "How can this belief be beneficial in sharing Christ's salvation with nonbelievers?"

Response
(5 minutes)

Ask for responses to study guide item 18.

(If someone volunteered to draw the New Jerusalem, display that while discussing the description in study guide item 18.)

18. Read Matthew 6:20; John 14:1-6; and Revelation 21:1 to 22:5. On the lines below, write out the description of heaven and the New Jerusalem found in these passages. (Look for more than the appearance.)

_____

_____

_____

_____

_____

_____

_____

_____

_____

_____

Discussion
(3 minutes)

Before asking for responses to study guide item 19, have a volunteer read aloud the description of *glory* or *glorified* in the word study reference book you brought to the session. Take a little time to discuss this definition and then have group members relate it to their responses to study guide item 19.

19. According to the following passages, what will be the condition of the Christian once in heaven? (Matthew 13:43, Romans 8:17, 2 Corinthians 4:17, Ephesians 1:18, Philippians 3:21, Colossians 3:4, 2 Timothy 2:10, and Revelation 22:5.)

_____

_____

_____

_____

_____

On earth all things must someday end. In eternity all things never end. The sinner's torment in hell never stops. Neither does the Christian's glorification in heaven. Hopefully the reality of this truth will cause us to act. When we speak of sin and salvation, of hell and heaven, we deal with eternal matters.

SUMMARY

Summary
(1 minute)
Remind group members to seek out the individual with whom they determined earlier in the session to share Christ.

Although God has judged every individual to be guilty of sin, He has a plan that will allow individuals to have a relationship with Him and receive the ultimate reward of sharing eternity with Him. We all need salvation and He has provided a way for us to accept His offering.

Through faith in Jesus Christ and repentance of sins, God gives us new life. This new life is a spiritual life. Through this regeneration, God justifies us and declares us to be righteous. His gift is offered to all people with no exceptions. Despite Satan's attempts to show Him otherwise, God is patient and loving, not wishing that any individual should die without coming into relationship with Him. He would like to have all His creation spend eternity with Him.

Heaven is a wonderful goal toward which we must travel each day of our lives. Let's live with eternity's values in view. Let's remember the unending glory that will be ours in that place and do our best to bring other lost souls with us to heaven

LET'S REVIEW

 1. In what ways do people sin?

_____

_____

_____

_____

 2. What is contained in the salvation that God has provided?

_____

_____

_____

_____

 3. Define *propitiation.*

_____

_____

_____

 4. What does *redemption* mean?

_____

_____

_____

_____

 5. With what did Christ redeem us?

_____

_____

_____

 6. Describe the final reward for a Christian.

_____

_____

_____

_____

 Review
(3 minutes)

Select two or three study guide items from the "Let's Review" section to review the material in this study. If comprehension seems lacking, suggest individuals reread the study.

Closing Prayer
(unlimited)

Ask if any in the group want to make a salvation decision. Pray with those who wish to do so. If there are none who are interested, pray for the millions who have never heard the salvation message and specifically for friends and family members of those in the group.

Preparing For Next Session

Remind group members to complete study 3 before the next session.

Arrange for your pastor or another individual who helps with water baptism in your church to share briefly with group members your church's requirements for water baptism. Let the spokesperson know that some in the group might be interested in baptism after this session. If they are unavailable, try to find out as much about it as you can so that you can share this information.

Group Fellowship
(5 minutes)

Encourage everyone to have refreshments and fellowship together before leaving.

Give a friendly reminder to those who volunteered to bring refreshments to the next session.

Study Objective

To discover the purpose and power of water baptism and take a stand for Christ by following through with being baptized.

What You Will Need

☐ A copy of resource 3A, "Why Water Baptism?" for each group member.
☐ An overhead projector.
☐ An overhead transparency of resource 3B, "Identifying With Christ."
☐ A Strong's Concordance. If you don't personally own a copy, ask your pastor to loan you his copy.
☐ Your pastor, or another informed individual, to share your church's requirements for water baptism at the end of the session.

Getting The Group's Attention

(All times are estimates. 7 minutes)

Have group members brainstorm about items, activities, and anything else that people do or wear to identify themselves with a group, individual, or club. Discuss what motivates people to choose to identify in these ways.

Ask individuals the following questions:

1. "Based on this, why is water baptism such an important action for Christians?"

2. "What should be our motivation for water baptism?"

WATER BAPTISM

The Christian life is basically one of obedience. One command Jesus gave just before His ascension was that His disciples practice and teach water baptism (Matthew 28:19). In light of this, water baptism is not optional.

One of the first things a Christian wants to do is let others know of the change that has occurred in his or her life. One of the ways to make a public testimony is by being obedient to Jesus' command to be baptized in water. But water baptism is also a deeply spiritual rite that has meaning far beyond the testimony given. It is meaningless unless it is the act of one who has accepted the Lord Jesus Christ as Savior.

Transition Statement ⇨   Water baptism identifies the believer with Christ.

COMMANDED BY JESUS

The practice of water baptism reaches back to the very foundation of the Christian Church, for it is one of two things Christ commanded all believers to observe. Historically, Protestants have recognized water baptism and the Lord's Supper as ordinances. In its broadest sense, the term *ordinance* simply means "a thing commanded or ordained." In the Church, an ordinance is a commandment given by Christ which all believers must follow.

For the Early Church, the idea of water baptism was not entirely new. It was a Jewish custom to baptize Gentiles who became converts to Judaism. And, immediately prior to Jesus' ministry, John the Baptist prepared the way for Christ by calling for persons to be baptized in water.

✎ **1. Read Mark 1:4; Luke 3:3,21; and Acts 19:4. What was the purpose of John the Baptist's baptism? Who took part in this baptism?**

_____

_____

✎ **2. Read John 1:26,27,29-34. What is said about John's baptism in this passage?**

_____

_____

_____

The baptism in water as practiced by John and the baptism in water as commanded by Jesus had different meanings.

✎ **3. Read Acts 19:2-5. How does this account make it evident that the two baptisms were not the same?**

_____

_____

_____

This is the only recorded instance of rebaptizing. It was necessary to demonstrate the difference between the baptism of John and the baptism of Jesus. John's baptism preceded salvation as a symbol of sincere repentance; Christ's followed salvation as a symbol of the believer's identification with Him.

PRACTICED BY THE APOSTLES

The commandment Jesus gave to His apostles in Matthew 28:19,20, was spoken at the time of His ascension to heaven. After Christ disappeared into heaven the apostles returned to Jerusalem to await the coming of the Holy Spirit. When the Holy Spirit filled the disciples (Acts 2:1-4), a great crowd gathered to see what the commotion was about, then lingered as they heard the disciples glorify God in other tongues.

Although the apostles had done some baptizing during the ministry of Jesus (John 3:22; 4:1,2), the first baptizing by the apostles after the commandment of Jesus seems to have taken place at Pentecost, 10 days after the ascension of Jesus. The multitude that gathered while the disciples spoke in tongues also heard Peter's sermon, explaining what was happening, and why.

⊥ **Lecture**
(3 minutes)
Present the material in the parallel column concerning ordinances and early practices of water baptism.

Open up the session for discussion of these ideas.

▨ **Response**
(4 minutes)
Have group members share their responses to study guide items 1 and 2.

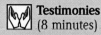
Testimonies
(8 minutes)

Have an individual share his or her response to study guide item 4.

Ask a few volunteers to share their water baptism experience. Have them discuss the process (waiting period, indoctrination classes, etc.) through which they had to go before being baptized.

Handout
(6 minutes)

Distribute a copy of resource 3A, "Why Water Baptism?" to each individual. Give group members 4 minutes to complete the work sheet.

Discuss how the example of the baptisms in these Scripture passages can direct our behavior.

Overhead
(5 minutes)

Display the transparency of resource 3B, "Identifying With Christ." Uncover and discuss each point as you come to it in the material in the parallel column and continuing through the next few pages.

4. Read Acts 2:37-41. What precedent was set following Peter's sermon?

_____

_____

How many followed Christ in this manner on that day? _____

This was just the beginning of following through with Christ's command. Other disciples baptized converts as well.

5. Read Acts 8:13; 8:36-38; 9:18; 16:14,15,31-34; 18:8; and 1 Corinthians 1:14-16. List on the lines below the incidents of baptism recorded in these passages. (Who baptized and who was baptized?) What requirement for Christian baptism is made clear by these passages?

_____

_____

_____

_____

_____

_____

_____

_____

6. Read Acts 10:47,48. What is revealed about the availability of water baptism?

_____

_____

_____

Paul's words indicate that water baptism is a privilege which should not be denied to any true believer. Christ's words concerning water baptism, its faithful practice by the Early Church, and the many references to it in the Epistles indicate the importance God places on water baptism. It is a fulfillment of the commandment of Jesus.

NEEDED BY BELIEVERS

The Meaning Of Water Baptism

We see the reason for the Lord's emphasis of water baptism when we understand its true meaning. It is a picture or representation of a spiritual truth. Baptism in water is a representation of the identification or union of the believer with Christ.

There are many Scripture passages that clarify the relationship of water baptism to the Christian's identification with Christ. Perhaps Romans 6:1-11 gives the most complete picture. So how do we identify with Christ through water baptism? There are several ways.

Baptism shows that the believer is identified with Christ in His crucifixion. Stepping forward to take part in water baptism is a physical demonstration of what the Bible says in several passages.

✎ **7. Read Romans 6:1,2,6 and Galatians 2:20; 5:24; 6:14. According to these passages, in what way does the baptized person identify with Christ's crucifixion?**

_____

_____

_____

How, then, is this an important symbolic step for the Christian? _____

_____

Water baptism is an outward symbol of a believer's crucifixion of his or her old sinful self. It is a testimony that the old is gone and the new has been birthed.

Baptism shows that the believer is identified with Christ in His death. (See Romans 6:3.) Christ died for us because of sin. We die to sin because of Christ. The individual who accepts Jesus as Savior is baptized by the Holy Spirit into the body of Christ (1 Corinthians 12:13). Baptism in water is a picture of that baptism into the body of Christ.

Baptism shows that the believer is identified with Christ in His burial. The believer's past with its sins and disgraces are all buried.

✎ **8. Read Romans 6:4 and Colossians 2:12. How does the Christian demonstrate identification with Christ's burial?**

_____

_____

The believer enters the grave with Christ. By voluntarily accepting Christ's death in his or her place, and by identifying with Christ's burial, the Christian testifies that his or her own sinful life has brought about the need for death and burial. The believer is buried with the Lord. We need to carefully consider this truth because too many persons today attempt to become Christians by merely using the name of Christ without assuming the responsibilities of that name. We follow Jesus into the waters of baptism to indicate that we are crucified, dead, and buried with the Lord Jesus Christ.

Water baptism shows that the believer is identified with Christ in His resurrection. The Christian life involves far more than crucifixion, death, and burial of self and sin. It also includes resurrection!

✎ **9. Read Romans 6:5,8; 2 Corinthians 4:14; Ephesians 2:4-6; and Colossians 2:12. For what reason are we given this resurrection?**

_____

_____

If we identify ourselves with Christ's humiliation and suffering, we can also expect to enjoy the same resurrection life He experienced. When we crucify ourselves, we do live, but in reality it is Christ living in us (Galatians 2:20). To be resurrected with Christ is also called "being quickened" or "made alive." It is a spiritual resurrection which provides power for victorious living. The Christian can testify that he or she was never alive to spiritual things, nor to true joy and satisfaction, until he or she accepted Christ as Savior.

✎ **10. Read 1 Thessalonians 4:16,17. What is the final display of this resurrection of believers?**

_____

Baptism shows that the believer is identified with Christ in His walk in newness of life. Before becoming a Christian a person is following the vain thoughts of his or her own mind; understanding is darkened because of separation from the life of God. Because of this, the sinner's way of life is entirely different from what God wants and expects. This person is uneasy in church, dislikes gospel services, and feels most comfortable around people who are unsaved.

✎ 11. Read Romans 6:4; Ephesians 4:22-24; and Colossians 2:6. What happens to a sinner after repenting and giving his or her life to God?

_____

_____

_____

Where and with whom might the new Christian feel most comfortable? _____

_____

_____

When the Christian emerges from the waters of baptism, he or she arises to embrace a new lifestyle. It is important not to go back to what used to be his or her normal lifestyle. Water baptism symbolizes a complete change of life aim. The person entering the water symbolizes the sinner who comes to identify himself or herself with Christ's crucifixion, death, and burial. The person emerging from the water symbolizes the spiritual resurrection and new life which Christ gives to him or her. So water baptism is far more than a testimony. It is a dramatization of the whole change that occurs in a saved person's life.

◨ **Response**
(2 minutes)
Have group members share their responses to study guide item 12.

✎ 12. Read Colossians 2:10,12,13. How does Paul describe what we gain through salvation and following Christ in baptism?

_____

_____

_____

The Manner Of Water Baptism

The question often arises, "What is the scriptural manner of baptism?" The believer wants to follow the Lord's instructions, but sees many different religious organizations practicing different methods of baptism. Some groups sprinkle water on the candidate for baptism. Others pour water on the person. Still others immerse the individual in the water. But what do the Scriptures teach?

✎ 13. Read Mark 1:9,10; John 3:23; and Acts 8:38,39. What manner of baptism is indicated in these passages?

_____

_____

_____

The English word *baptism* is a transliteration of the Greek word *baptisma*. That is to say, we have made the Greek word into an English word. So, wherever the English word *baptism* occurs in the New Testament, it represents the Greek word *baptisma*, and preserves the same meaning as the Greek word.

The Greek word, *baptisma*, is based upon another Greek word, *bapto*, which means "I dip" or "I dye." It is used in three instances in the New Testament.

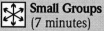 14. Read Luke 16:24, John 13:26, and Revelation 19:13. The Greek word *bapto* is used in each of these verses. What meaning of the word is disclosed?

_____

_____

_____

If *baptism* is derived from the Greek *baptisma* or *bapto*, what conclusion can be drawn concerning the biblical manner of water baptism?

_____

_____

_____

Another important part of the manner of baptism is found in Jesus' command to His disciples just before His ascension.

 15. Read Matthew 28:19. Concerning baptism, what was Jesus' command?

_____

_____

This is a recognition that the Triune Godhead participated in the salvation of every person. Also, a correct translation of the Greek is to baptize converts "into" the name of the Father, Son, and Holy Spirit. We are baptized "into" fellowship with the name of the Holy Trinity.

 16. Read Acts 2:38. How can Paul's statement be reconciled with Jesus' command?

_____

_____

_____

_____

One is the formula and one is the authority by which all are baptized. Acknowledging Jesus to be Christ and Lord is the reason and purpose of baptism.

SUMMARY

Water baptism is a symbol of believers turning away from their old sinful lives and following Christ in all ways. It is an outward show of giving themselves to God through faith in Jesus Christ. It demonstrates the stages of crucifying their old self, dying to the things of the flesh, putting past sins behind them, rising anew through the power of God, and walking in relationship with Jesus.

Water baptism doesn't grant salvation but gives testimony of it. It does not rid us of our old selves, but signifies the being rid of it. It is a natural step to take after becoming a believer. Water baptism is one way in which a Christian can live in obedience to Christ, since He commanded us to do so (Matthew 28:19).

The practice of water baptism had been around for quite some time before Jesus stated to His disciples that they should make disciples themselves and baptize them. But the ordinance as we know it began at the point of the Church's first major growth spurt—the Day of Pentecost. Three thousand new believers were baptized after listening to Peter's sermon. We need to continue to follow Him in water baptism, demonstrating our dying to ourselves and allowing Him to live through us.

Small Groups
(7 minutes)

Have group members gather into smaller groups of three or four and discuss their responses to study guide item 14. Give them 4 minutes.

Have everyone regather into the larger group. Have different ones share the results of their discussions. Be prepared to share a definition of *bapto* out of the Strong's Concordance (Greek dictionary section, entry number 911) you brought to the session.

Response
(3 minutes)

Have group members share their responses to study guide item 16.

Correction — Q16
Paul's s/b
Peter's

Discussion
(5 minutes)

Let your pastor or other individual talk with the group regarding specific requirements for water baptism in your church. Allow those who wish to be baptized to talk with the pastor and make arrangements for it. (If it is necessary for you to share this information with the group, be sure to give the names of those who wish to be baptized and their questions to the pastor.)

Review
(3 minutes)

Select two or three study guide items from the "Let's Review" section to check the comprehension level of group members. If understanding of the study material seems weak, recommend that individuals work through the study again.

 Closing Prayer
(2 minutes)

Ask an individual to close the session in prayer, thanking God for the opportunity to "stand up" for Him through water baptism. Have him or her pray for those who have not yet been water baptized.

 Preparing For Next Session

Remind group members to complete study 4 before the next session.

Arrange for two individuals to each make a 3-minute report on a successful actor/actress, athlete, or businessperson who has had to work very hard for his or her success. Have them find out each person's methods for success in his or her field.

Arrange for a group member to make a 3- to 5-minute report on Satan including his different names and their meaning, his origin, his activity now, and his future. Suggest that the individual use a Bible encyclopedia and other reference books to find the information.

 Group Fellowship
(5 minutes)

Invite individuals to share in fellowship and refreshments before they leave.

LET'S REVIEW

1. What does *ordinance* mean? What is a Church ordinance?

_____

_____

_____

2. When did Jesus command water baptism?

_____

_____

3. Was water baptism a completely new idea to the apostles? Explain.

_____

_____

4. How was the baptism which Jesus commanded different from the baptism practiced by John the Baptist?

_____

_____

_____

_____

5. In what ways does baptism illustrate the believer's identification with Christ?

_____

_____

_____

_____

6. What is the biblical manner and formula of water baptism?

_____

_____

_____

_____

VICTORIOUS LIVING

What do we mean by the phrase "a victorious Christian life"? Perhaps we can understand better by way of contrast. A defeated Christian is insecure, constantly yielding to temptations, and unhappy. He or she does not have peace because a spiritual fight is still going on within. A defeated Christian has not yielded completely to God.

Victory is not an elusive quality which is beyond our grasp, but neither can we gain it by our own efforts. Victorious Christians have learned a wonderful secret. The way to power over sin, temptation, and self is by claiming Christ's victory over Satan as their own. True victorious living means complete identification with Christ. Yielded to Him, the child of God enjoys the actual victories Christ purchased on the cross.

Complete reliance on God will lead to a victorious Christian life.

⊙ Study Objective

To evaluate the basis for living a victorious Christian life and commit to relying on Christ to be our victory over the powers of darkness.

✓ What You Will Need

☐ Two individuals to make a 3-minute report as outlined on page 30 of this leader's guide.

☐ A group member to make a 3- to 5-minute report on Satan as outlined on page 30 of this leader's guide.

☐ Enough copies of resource 4A, "G-R-A-C-E," for each group member.

☐ An overhead projector and transparencies and/or a marker board and appropriate markers.

☐ An overhead transparency of resource 4B, "How To Be A Victorious Christian."

▽ Getting The Group's Attention

(All times are estimates. 10 minutes)

Have the prepared group members give their success story reports. Ask the rest of the group to note any methods for success followed by either individual.

Following the reports, ask group members to suggest ways the methods for success presented can be used by us to become winners as Christians. Have a volunteer record the suggestions.

After 2 minutes, have a volunteer read 1 Corinthians 9:24-27 aloud. Ask individuals to discuss how Paul's comments relate to yielding fully to God and His will and, therefore, to gaining a victorious life.

⇦ Transition Statement

GOD'S PROVISION

The victorious work of Christ has always been part of the eternal plan of God. His victory over Satan and the powers of darkness was foreseen by God. To understand victorious Christian living, one must look at the enemy who attempts to keep us from victory. Christ defeated him on the cross, but why was that necessary?

✎ 1. Read Isaiah 14:12-15 and Ezekiel 28:16,17. What is revealed about Satan in these passages?

_____

_____

_____

What sin was attributed to him? _____

What was God's response? _____

_____

Satan was not always an enemy of God. But he took things given him by God to be used for good and corrupted them to create something evil and unclean. God did not create sin; Satan is the author of sin.

Later God again pronounced the outcome of Satan. This occurred after Satan tempted Eve, provoking her and Adam to sin.

✎ 2. Read Genesis 3:15 and Luke 23:44-46; 24:1-7. What judgment did God pronounce on Satan in this verse?

_____

_____

How was the prophecy given in the Genesis account fulfilled in the Luke accounts?

_____

_____

This was another opportunity to disclose His eternal plan for humankind. He knew who would be victorious in the end, from the beginning.

Christ came to earth with one distinct purpose. He came to deliver people from their bondage to Satan.

✎ 3. Read Romans 5:6; Galatians 4:4,5; and Hebrews 2:14,15. What is stated about the timing of Christ's coming to earth?

_____

_____

_____

For what purpose did He become a man and live with us? (See also 1 John 3:8.)

_____

_____

_____

On the cross, Jesus Christ completely defeated Satan by paying in full the penalty for sin for all humanity. He totally destroyed Satan's power and influence.

✎ **4. Read John 8:34 and Romans 6:16. How do people enslave themselves to Satan?**

_____

_____

_____

Christ came to bring freedom to people who are in slavery to Satan. His victory over Satan was complete. He stripped him and his demons of all power. Colossians 2:15 tells us that He made public displays of them. But Christ did not intend to keep His victory for himself only. He came to share it. In Christ's victory, Satan and his forces were forever made powerless against Him and all those who believe in Him.

✎ **5. Read 2 Timothy 1:10. What else did Christ bring to those who would believe in Him?**

_____

_____

Sin had brought death into the world. Jesus came to render ineffective the one who had the power of death. He was victorious over both. He eliminated our debt. Those persons who will accept Christ's victory as their own, who will completely identify themselves with Jesus, and who will stop attempting to win the fight with Satan in their own strength, will find a new place of victory in the Lord Jesus Christ.

PERSONAL EXPERIENCE

Satan continually tries to make the Christian look at himself and his shortcomings rather than to Jesus and His victory. The basis for victorious Christian living is found in the Christian's union with Christ. The person who is united with Jesus finds that Christ's victory over Satan is his or her victory. Satan is powerless against such a person.

Many people who believe in Christ do not realize the comprehensive nature of the victory which they have in Christ. These people try to live victoriously by their own efforts. These attempts are very sincere but if their source of strength is only within themselves, they cannot succeed. Individuals who try to find victory in this way will be sure to give in to temptation or seek to justify themselves with self-made rules and regulations.

✎ **6. Read Colossians 2:20-23. What does the Bible say about those who live according to human rules?**

_____

_____

_____

_____

Though human rules may have some merit, they will not keep the Christian from yielding to Satan's more subtle and less obvious temptations—temptations that can create a great amount of damage to the Christian's life.

✎ **7. Read 1 Corinthians 15:57. From where does our victory come?**

_____

_____

_____

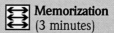

Memorization
(3 minutes)
Have a volunteer look up 1 John 4:4. Write the verse out

1 John 4:4 - Ye are of God... and have overcome them; because Greater is He that is in you, than he that is in the world.

rization.)

Small Groups
(10 minutes)
Have the group divide into groups of four or five. Have each group read 1 Corinthians 10:13 and 2 Corinthians 12:9 and identify the provisions for Christians which are spoken of in these verses.

Give the groups 4 minutes to complete this, then ask the whole group, "So what is our basis for victory?"

While group members are still in their smaller groups, have each group define *grace*. Distribute a copy of resource 4A, "G-R-A-C-E," to each individual. Give the smaller groups 3 minutes to work together to create an acrostic for the word *grace* and share it with the larger group. Allow a little time to let each group share its acrostic.

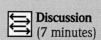

Discussion
(7 minutes)
Have group members share their responses to study guide item 6. Have three volunteers look up and read aloud Isaiah 64:6, Romans 10:3, and Philippians 3:9. Ask individuals the following questions:

1. "What does God say about human beings' attempts at righteousness?"

2. "How do human rules and attempts at righteousness go together?"

3. "What, instead, should be our source of righteousness?"

Have group members share their responses to study guide item 8.

8. Read Romans 6:8-14. How was spiritual victory accomplished and how is it ours?

_____

_____

_____

_____

God has given us the wonderful promise of victory. The key to victorious living is not daily resolve to overcome this or that sin. In fact, that attitude brings the sin too much to the mind of the believer. The secret of victory is to yield completely to Christ, to fill the mind with the things of God, and to remain open to the leading of the Holy Spirit.

The person who is caught up in the sin of loving money more than anything cannot gain victory over it by just gritting his or her teeth and determining to stop wanting money. There must be a conscious act of focusing on heavenly riches; seeing that heaven is near, life is short, and eternity is unending. To be truly wealthy this individual must lead people to Christ and invest in God's work. As God makes these truths real, this person will find complete victory over the love of money. A greater love for God will replace a lesser love for worldly possessions. In this way, he or she gains victory.

We can accomplish victory by realizing that we are truly dead to our sinful lives but alive in God through the work of Jesus Christ. We are not only dead with Christ; we are also risen with Christ. Through this identification in the resurrection of Christ, sin is made powerless over the believer.

9. Read Colossians 3:1-3. What responsibility does the Christian have to live victoriously?

_____

_____

_____

All believers make this choice. Either the things of God or the things of this world will occupy our minds.

10. Paul gave specific instruction concerning victorious living. Read Romans 6:12,13. What is indicative of the victorious life?

_____

_____

_____

_____

Discussion
(3 minutes)

Have several individuals share their responses to study guide item 10. Ask, "In what practical ways can we follow the direction of this passage?"

Obedience to rules and regulations of humankind does not prove that individuals are living victoriously. Some people have taken the attitude that since Christ supplies the victory, they need do nothing. They feel that any effort on their part is a work of the flesh. This attitude is entirely wrong. Each believer has a will. Individuals control their own lives and guide their own decisions every day. They decide whether or not to let Jesus rule their lives. Victorious Christian living is like boarding a train. The train does the work; it carries the passengers at a speed far faster than they could run. But the passengers decide whether or not to board. Thus Christians who live victoriously do so by the strength and power of Jesus Christ, but believers choose whether or not to claim this victory.

A person demonstrates yieldedness to God in practical Christian living. The person who is yielded to God does not yield to sin.

11. Read Colossians 3:5-9. In order to live in victory, what must we do?

_____

_____

_____

These are not the products of a victorious life. If our lives contain these things we have not yet let Christ live in and through us as He can. We are not living victoriously unless our lives show the fruit of Christ's victory. Christians must not fall into the modern-day trap that refuses to recognize or admit the presence of sin. People who are dead to sin cannot live in sin. Dead to sin, they put the sins in their lives to death. We must be realists. If our lives contain sin, God wants to remove it. Let us permit Him to do so.

One of the marvels of Christianity is its power to change lives. The victorious Christian's life is a testimony to the transforming ability of Christ.

 12. Read 2 Corinthians 5:17 and Ephesians 4:22-24. What happens when someone becomes a Christian?

_____

 13. Read Colossians 3:12-15. What evidences of a victorious life should we display?

_____

_____

_____

_____

Victorious living involves a spiritual change of clothing. Christ has given us a gift of spiritual apparel which we are to "put on." When we first received that gift, how anxious we were to try it on! How much we desired to see how the new clothing would look on us. Yet some of us have never put on this new clothing.

Christ has given us the new clothing. We have accepted it and He expects that we wear it. We may even have unwrapped the gift and opened its box. But have we ever put on the new apparel? If not, why not? Is it because perhaps we hate to strip ourselves of the filthy rags of the old life which we have been wearing? Before we can "put on" the new, we must first "put off" the old. With the new clothing at our disposal, it is strange that we have stubbornly refused to remove the old clothing in order that we might put on the new. To live victoriously, we must simply change our spiritual clothing. When we have "put off" the old and have "put on" the new, we will find that we can live victoriously.

SUMMARY

The victorious Christian recognizes that his or her life is actually Christ's. The believer is united with Christ in His glorious victory over Satan. He or she is a new creation, free from the domination of sin because of that victory. There is no excuse for not living victoriously. The Christ-life is a victorious life, a life transformed through Christ and the indwelling Holy Spirit of God. All that is necessary is that the believer use the power for victorious living which has been made available in the resurrection of Jesus Christ. The Christian merely needs to begin to live like the victor he or she already is.

Satan claims that the victorious life is impossible. But God says it is ours to claim, if we will. It is a life of Christlikeness; a life created anew from the ruins of past failures; a life formed by the power of the indwelling Son of God. None of the defeats we have suffered in our Christian walk prove that a victorious life is impossible. Instead, they merely show that victory through our own efforts is impossible.

We have victory. Victory through Jesus Christ our Lord!

Discussion
(7 minutes)
Have group members share their responses to study guide items 11-13. Ask, "What role does self-discipline play in developing the evidences of a victorious life, and how does it differ from self-righteousness?"

 Summary
(3 minutes)
Display resource 4B, "How To Be A Victorious Christian." Recap the session by highlighting the four basic elements which lead to a victorious life. Encourage group members to release themselves fully to the guidance and direction of God.

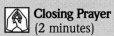

Review
(3 minutes)

Select two or three study guide items from the "Let's Review" section to review the material in this study. If comprehension seems lacking, suggest individuals reread the study.

Closing Prayer
(2 minutes)

Close the session by asking everyone to consider his or her life and level of commitment to God. Pray that each member will begin to rely completely on Christ for strength to face every trial and hardship.

Preparing For Next Session

Remind individuals to complete study 5 before the next session.

Arrange for a group member to make a 3-minute report comparing and contrasting Charismatics and Pentecostals.

Group Fellowship
(5 minutes)

Encourage everyone to have refreshments and fellowship together before leaving.

1. Why was the victory of Christ over Satan necessary?

_____

_____

_____

_____

2. What caused Satan to rebel against God who created him?

_____

_____

_____

_____

3. What is it that brings people into the slavery of Satan?

_____

_____

_____

_____

4. What responsibility does the Christian have to live victoriously?

_____

_____

_____

_____

5. How does a person show that he or she is yielded to God?

_____

_____

_____

_____

_____

STUDY 5

BAPTISM IN THE HOLY SPIRIT

God has promised a wonderful gift to all believers, but the tragedy is that many Christians have never received what He offers. His gift is the baptism in the Holy Spirit.

The distinguishing mark of the Pentecostal movement is our belief in the baptism in the Holy Spirit with the initial evidence of speaking in tongues. We believe that this Baptism was not only for the Church in apostolic days but it is intended for all believers through all time. We believe the Lord baptizes in the Holy Spirit today just as He did during the first Christian century, empowering His children for a ministry of witnessing.

More than ever before believers need to be empowered super-naturally by the Holy Spirit. Christian witnesses are being confronted by organized satanic efforts throughout the world bent on hindering the work of Christ. Only Spirit-filled men and women can adequately cope with this situation and emerge from the conflict victoriously.

⊙ **Study Objective**

To comprehend the importance of being baptized in the Holy Spirit and seek to be baptized or have a fresh outpouring of the Spirit's power in our lives.

☑ **What You Will Need**

☐ An overhead projector, blank transparency, and marker.
☐ An overhead transparency of resources 5A, "The Holy Spirit," and 5B, "Who Can Be Baptized In the Holy Spirit?"

⧖ **Getting The Group's Attention**

(All times are estimates. 10 minutes)

Display resource 5A, "The Holy Spirit." Have volunteers look up and read aloud each of the Scripture passages listed on the transparency. Next to each reference write out how the Holy Spirit is described in that particular passage.

Ask, "From these passages, why is the Holy Spirit so important to the Christian?"

The baptism in the Holy Spirit provides power to be mighty witnesses for Christ.

⬒ Transition Statement

Some people seem to think that the Holy Spirit baptism is simply a doctrine accepted by some and rejected by others. But the baptism in the Holy Spirit is a promise given by the Father. It is a basic teaching of the Bible.

✎ 1. Read Joel 2:28-32. Using a study Bible, determine approximately how long before the Day of Pentecost was the Holy Spirit promised by the Father?

_____

Quite a few years passed before the coming of the Holy Spirit on Pentecost. But these were not wasted years. During these years God prepared the way for the fulfillment of the promise. Before He sent the Holy Spirit, it was His plan to send the Son.

✎ 2. Read Luke 24:49 and Acts 1:4. Based on these verses, why was it part of God's plan to send the Son before He sent the Holy Spirit?

_____

_____

Jesus was involved in announcing the coming of the Holy Spirit in another way also. He promised to send the Holy Spirit.

✎ 3. Read John 14:16-18. At what point and for what purpose did Jesus promise His disciples the Holy Spirit?

_____

_____

Later Jesus even stated that it would be better for the disciples when He left because then they would have the Holy Spirit with them always. Clearly, He felt it was important for them to have this promised gift.

When Jesus rose from the dead, just before His ascension to heaven, He once again promised the coming of the Holy Spirit. (See Luke 24:49 and Acts 1:8.)

In His references to the coming of the Holy Spirit, Jesus indicated that some conditions had to be fulfilled before the Holy Spirit could come.

❍ *People had to be ready for His coming.* This was necessary because the world is unable to receive the Holy Spirit because it is unable to see or know Him. (See John 14:17.) As the life of Jesus on earth drew toward its close, a people had been made ready for the coming of the Holy Spirit. The believers were looking for His coming.

❍ *Jesus had to ascend to the Father.*

✎ 4. Read John 16:7. Why was it necessary for Jesus to ascend to the Father before the coming of the Holy Spirit?

_____

_____

_____

_____

❍ *The disciples had to wait at Jerusalem.* Jesus made it clear at the Ascension that the disciples were to wait in Jerusalem until they received the Holy Spirit. He knew they were not prepared to be the witnesses He needed. The disciples were obedient and waited about 10 days before the Holy Spirit descended upon them on that first Pentecost.

Discussion
(5 minutes)

Have group members share their responses to study guide items 1 and 2.

Have a volunteer read Acts 1:5. Ask the following questions:

1. "To whom was Jesus speaking in this verse?"

2. "What does this verse indicate about the timing of receiving the gift of salvation and the gift of the Holy Spirit?"

Small Groups
(8 minutes)

Have group members gather into groups of four or five. Have each group discuss for 5 minutes the following questions based on Acts 2:1-21 and be prepared to share the results of its discussion with the larger group.

1. "What do you think the 120 expected as they waited in the Upper Room? Do you think they expected to speak with other tongues? Why or why not?"

2. "How did Peter know that what was happening was a fulfillment of Joel's prophecy?" (See Joel 2:28-32.)

Have a representative from each group share its findings. Encourage friendly discussion as each group shares.

THE PURPOSE

God had a purpose in baptizing the members of the Early Church in the Holy Spirit. This purpose is stated twice before Jesus' ascension.

✎ **5. Read Luke 24:49 and Acts 1:8. What was the purpose of Jesus and the Father in baptizing the members of the Early Church in the Holy Spirit?**

_____

_____

_____

Often the baptism in the Holy Spirit is accompanied by a wonderful experience of the nearness of God. The joy the Spirit-filled believer receives is marvelous and may become the center of conversation whenever he or she speaks of the experience. But Jesus made it clear that the power of the Holy Spirit was what the disciples needed.

✎ **6. Read Luke 24:46-48. Of what were the members of the Early Church to be witnesses?**

_____

_____

Notice the change in Peter after he received the Holy Spirit.

✎ **7. Read Matthew 26:74; John 20:19; and Acts 2:14-40. Give a brief description of Peter before being baptized in the Holy Spirit and after. Identify the change in his actions.**

_____

_____

_____

_____

_____

The baptism in the Holy Spirit is not a limited experience. When brought before the Sanhedrin for healing and preaching repentance and remission of sins, Peter boldly testified to them. He was a part of the first "missionary" outreach.

✎ **8. Read John 16:14. How does Jesus' statement about the Holy Spirit match up with the purpose of power for witnessing?**

_____

_____

_____

It is interesting that those churches where the Holy Spirit is honored and given place in the service are also strongly evangelistic. Those Christians who are baptized in the Holy Spirit have a greater zeal for souls. The purpose of Holy Spirit baptism is the same today as it was in the days of the Early Church—power for witnessing.

Response
(5 minutes)
Have group members share their responses to study guide items 5-7.

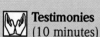

Testimonies
(10 minutes)
Allow several individuals who have received the baptism in the Spirit to testify. Have each specifically identify the following:
✔ What he or she expected to feel when baptized in the Spirit;
✔ what he or she actually felt;
✔ how he or she would encourage others seeking the Baptism;
✔ how the Baptism has impacted or changed his or her life.

Presentation
(4 minutes)
Present the individual prepared to give the report comparing and contrasting charismatics and Pentecostals. Allow a minute or so for discussion following the presentation.

Pentecostals believe that the initial evidence of being baptized in the Spirit is speaking in other tongues. By "speaking in other tongues" we mean the supernatural empowerment to speak a language unknown and unlearned by the speaker.

Why do Pentecostals set such an impossible sign as the evidence of being baptized in the Spirit? A more subjective evidence—such as being joyful or "blessed"—would be more within the reach of seekers. The answer is found in the Bible. Pentecostals believe that the baptism in the Holy Spirit is a supernatural experience and that believers are actually filled by God the Holy Spirit. When this occurs, the individual speaks in other tongues as the Spirit enables him or her. The history of the Early Church gives several examples of Holy Spirit baptism with speaking in tongues as the initial evidence.

❏ *The Example Of Pentecost.* About 120 believers were gathered together at Pentecost.

9. Read Acts 2:1-4. What evidences of the Holy Spirit are described in this passage?

_____

_____

_____

Discussion
(5 minutes)
Have five volunteers look up the Scripture references in each subhead and related study guide item in the parallel column, beginning with "The Example Of Pentecost" and continuing through "The Example Of Samaria."

After each passage has been read aloud, ask, "What evidence of Holy Spirit baptism is indicated in each example?"

❏ *The Example At Caesarea.* The Gentiles at Caesarea were baptized in the Holy Spirit. Peter went there to minister to these Gentiles unsure of what God was going to do. He and other Jewish brothers witnessed God's outpouring of the Holy Spirit on these Gentile believers.

10. Read Acts 10:44-46; 11:15-17; 15:8. By what evidence were Peter and his companions convinced these believers had been filled with the Spirit?

_____

In the chapter 11 and 15 references, what comment did Peter make regarding the Gentiles' Baptism experience?

_____

_____

❏ *The Example At Ephesus.* When the Ephesians were baptized in the Holy Spirit, they spoke with other tongues, just as the believers had at Jerusalem and at Caesarea. (See Acts 19:6.)

❏ *The Example Of Paul.* The apostle Paul was baptized with the Holy Spirit (Acts 9:17). This account in Acts does not state that he spoke in tongues at that particular time but it does say Ananias was sent to him so Paul may be filled with the Holy Spirit.

11. Read 1 Corinthians 14:18. What implication concerning Paul's baptism in the Holy Spirit is shared in this verse?

_____

_____

_____

We must remember that in the Early Church there was no controversy about whether or not a person should speak in tongues when he or she received the infilling of the Holy Spirit. Such an argument arises only when we view the Early Church experiences from the distance of 20 centuries.

❐ *The Example Of Samaria.* Peter and John prayed for the Samaritan believers that they might receive the Holy Spirit, and the record indicates that they did (Acts 8:15,17). Once again the account does not definitely state that there was evidence of speaking in tongues. Something marvelous and unique must have happened though to inspire Simon the sorcerer to want to buy the ability to give this gift (Acts 8:18,19). He and the other Samaritans had already seen miracles and healings take place (Acts 8:5-13). The receiving of the Holy Spirit by the Samaritan believers must have been evidenced by something amazing and different from what Simon had already seen. In light of the scriptural pattern, it probably was that the believers spoke in tongues as the Spirit gave them utterance.

❐ *The Final Evidence.* God bears witness to the baptism in the Spirit through the evidence of speaking in another language. He does it today, just as He did then. Hundreds of thousands of Pentecostals have received the Holy Spirit and have spoken in other tongues. While this is the first evidence of baptism in the Holy Spirit, there is another ultimate, evidence of Spirit baptism.

✎ 12. Read Acts 1:8; 5:29-32. What is the ultimate evidence of baptism in the Holy Spirit?

_____

_____

We must not be content with speaking in tongues alone as a sole evidence of baptism in the Holy Spirit. We must use the power given in Spirit baptism.

THE PROVISION

God has no favorites when He judges humankind; He has no favorites when He offers salvation; nor does He have favorites when He offers the baptism in the Holy Spirit.

✎ 13. Read Acts 2:38,39. For whom has God provided the baptism in the Holy Spirit?

_____

Is it limited to a particular time period? Explain. _____

_____

_____

God does not limit His baptism in the Holy Spirit; only humans draw limits. God has continued to baptize in the Spirit because He still wants Spirit-empowered witnesses. It is through His witnesses that He brings others into His Church.

SUMMARY

God gave the gift of the Holy Spirit to the Early Church because He knew they could not accomplish the task of evangelizing the world for Him without the power of the Spirit. He wants each of us to be baptized in the Holy Spirit so we too can be powerful witnesses for Him. He wants us to be witnesses to the sufferings, death, and resurrection of Christ. He wants us to be witnesses to the need of repentance and to forgiveness of sin through Jesus Christ.

The Holy Spirit has been given to help us in our witnessing for the Lord. Let us accept the gift of the Holy Spirit He is offering to us. Let us be baptized in the Holy Spirit. Let's not stop with the initial evidence of baptism in the Holy Spirit, but let's put to use the power we will receive to witness for Christ.

Response
(5 minutes)

Have group members share their responses to study guide item 12. Ask, "How else did God manifest His power in the disciples?" (Assist individuals by having volunteers read aloud the following: John 18:17,25-27; Acts 2:14,36-39; Acts 2:47; Acts 4:31-33; and Acts 7:54-60.)

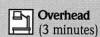

Overhead
(3 minutes)

Display the overhead transparency of resource 5B, "Who Can Be Baptized In the Holy Spirit?" Reveal each line as you read through Acts 2:39.

Brainstorm
(5 minutes)

State: "A church that is in one accord can still make a city sit up and take notice."

Ask, "What can we do to make our church so alive in the Spirit that our entire community and town will take notice?"

Record individuals' responses on a blank transparency. After 3 minutes, stop and have the group pray together for a revival to begin in your church.

Review
(3 minutes)

Select two or three study guide items from the "Let's Review" section to check the comprehension level of group members. If understanding of the study material seems weak, recommend that individuals work through the study again.

Closing Prayer
(unlimited)

Ask if any group members would like to pray for the baptism in the Holy Spirit. Have individuals who have already been baptized pray with any who are interested.

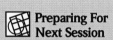
Preparing For Next Session

Remind group members to complete study 6 before the next session.

Prepare slips of paper with names of items to be identified by a sales pitch and another set of slips of paper with the names of items or activities to be drawn on them. (See page 43 for more details.)

Cut apart resource 6A, "Teamwork!" as specified on the work sheet.

Group Fellowship
(5 minutes)

Invite individuals to share in fellowship and refreshments before they leave.

LET'S REVIEW

1. When was the Holy Spirit promised by the Father? By Jesus?

_____

_____

_____

2. Why was it part of God's plan to send His Son before He sent the Holy Spirit?

_____

_____

_____

_____

3. What was the purpose of Jesus and the Father in baptizing the members of the Early Church in the Holy Spirit?

_____

_____

_____

4. Of what were the members of the Early Church to be witnesses?

_____

_____

_____

5. For whom has God provided the baptism in the Holy Spirit?

_____

_____

_____

6. Why has God continued to baptize in the Holy Spirit?

_____

_____

_____

_____

STUDY 6

GIFTS OF THE HOLY SPIRIT

Pentecostals believe that the gifts given by God to the Early Church are still available to believers today. The gifts of the Spirit are the divinely appointed means by which the power received at the time of Baptism is manifested through those who receive.

The primary purpose of the gifts of the Spirit is to edify or build up the Church, which is the body of Christ. The gifts are given by the Holy Spirit to individuals in the Church to be used for the good of all.

God has provided specific instructions as to how these gifts are to be used in chapters 12, 13, and 14 of 1 Corinthians. He desires that we be knowledgeable concerning the nature and operations of the gifts of the Spirit so we can avoid fanaticism and confusion in our ministry to one another.

The gifts of the Spirit are provided for and should be used for the benefit of the entire Church.

Study Objective

To explore the purpose of spiritual gifts and pray for the operation of these gifts within this group and the Church.

What You Will Need

☐ A copy of resource 6A, "Teamwork!" for each small group in the "Getting The Group's Attention" activity. Cut apart each portion of the activity. Keep the bottom portion with the answers on it.

☐ Two boxes—one with slips of paper with items to be pitched; and the other, slips with items to be drawn. (See the "Getting The Group's Attention" activity.)

☐ A marker board or several large pieces of paper and markers.

☐ An overhead projector.

☐ An overhead transparency of resource 6B, "The Gifts."

Getting The Group's Attention

(All times are estimates. 10 minutes)

Have the group divide into smaller groups of five to nine. Have each group select the group member best qualified to complete an activity in each of the categories listed on resource 6A, "Teamwork!"

Have the group member selected to make the sales pitch draw a slip of paper with a product name on it and make the pitch. As each group completes a portion of the activity, give them the next portion of resource 6A, "Teamwork!"

Allow 10 minutes for all teams to complete all the activities. Explain how the whole group benefits when the expertise of individuals is allowed to be expressed. In the same way when individuals express their spiritual gifts properly, the whole church benefits.

Transition Statement

THE PURPOSE OF THE GIFTS

God does not want us to be ignorant of the gifts of the Holy Spirit or how they are to be used. God grants the spiritual gifts to individuals for a specific purpose.

✎ 1. Read 1 Corinthians 12:7. What is the purpose for which God distributes the gifts of the Spirit?

_____

_____

If we remember this truth, we will recognize that any use of the spiritual gifts which is opposed to this truth is not of God. If we know the purpose of the gifts, it will help us to use the gifts correctly. We must also remember this as we seek after spiritual gifts (which is what God wants us to do—see 1 Corinthians 12:31); we must want them for the right purpose. Self-exaltation is not a proper motive for desiring gifts of the Spirit.

✎ 2. Read 1 Corinthians 12:4-6,12. What foundational principles concerning spiritual gifts and their use are revealed in this passage?

_____

_____

_____

_____

_____

The Holy Spirit has distributed different spiritual gifts to different members of the Body, but each gift is to be used by its possessor for the good of the whole body of Christ. Different persons are used for the manifestation of different gifts, but no one who is used in a particular way can say he or she is more important than another person. Since we are like a body, each supporting and providing for the other, each gift is to be used as a ministry which will benefit the entire Church, not just one or a few members.

THE NATURE OF THE GIFTS

Nine gifts of the Spirit are identified in 1 Corinthians 12:8-10.

✎ 3. Read 1 Corinthians 12:8-10. On the lines below list the spiritual gifts identified.

_____

_____

_____

_____

_____

_____

_____

Response
(5 minutes)
Have individuals share their responses to study guide items 1 and 2.

Overhead
(3 minutes)
Have a volunteer list the nine gifts as recorded in his or her response to study guide item 3.

Display the title of resource 6B, "The Gifts." Uncover each gift as you discuss the material in the parallel column of the next few pages of the study guide material.

These gifts of the Spirit may be classified in three categories:

(1) **Those that impart power to know supernaturally**—the word of wisdom, the word of knowledge, and the distinguishing between spirits.

(2) **Those that impart power to act supernaturally**—faith, healing, and miracles.

(3) **Those that impart power to speak supernaturally**—prophecy, tongues, and interpretation of tongues.

Each of the spiritual gifts contributes to the welfare of the Church. They are all given by the same Spirit. Here is a brief definition of the gifts of the Spirit mentioned in the 1 Corinthians reference.

❐ *The Word Of Wisdom.* God has given this spiritual gift to some members of His Church to give guidance in a time of need. Those who exercise this gift speak the right word at the right time for the benefit of the Church.

✎ **4. Read Acts 15:13-22. Describe how the word of wisdom was used in this account. What was the benefit to the Church?**

_____

_____

_____

_____

❐ *The Word Of Knowledge.* This gift enables the Church to receive spiritual information which is needed.

✎ **5. Read Acts 5:1-11. Describe how the word of knowledge was used in this account. How did it benefit the Church?**

_____

_____

_____

_____

_____

❐ *Distinguishing Between Spirits.* This gift is to be used to determine whether or not an utterance is from the Holy Spirit. The Holy Spirit reveals what kind of spirit, holy or unholy, is in operation in a person's life or in a certain situation. It is not to test motives of other believers' actions.

✎ **6. Read Matthew 24:4,5; 1 Timothy 4:1; and 1 John 4:1. According to these passages, why has the gift of distinguishing between spirits always been important to the Church, and all the more so now?**

_____

_____

_____

_____

_____

Read
(4 minutes)
Have volunteers read Ephesians 4:11 and Romans 12:6-8. Ask, "Should these also be called gifts of the Spirit? Why or why not?"

Overhead
(6 minutes)
Uncover the first main heading and each of its subpoints, as you discuss them, on resource 6B. For further clarification of these gifts, have volunteers share their responses to the associated study guide items in the parallel column.

Uncover the second main heading and each of its sub-points, as you discuss them, on resource 6B. Once again, have individuals share their responses to the associated study guide items in the parallel column.

❐ *Faith.* The gift of faith is not a saving faith, but rather faith directed toward some special end—faith to do wonders.

7. Read Acts 3:1-10. How does this passage illustrate the gift of faith?

_____

_____

_____

_____

❐ *Gifts Of Healing.* For the physical welfare of the Church, God has given to certain members of the Body gifts of healing. The literal Greek translation indicates the plural, "healings," and this seems to imply that provision has been made for the healing of different kinds of sicknesses and diseases. Prayer for healing is not limited to those who have this gift. There are numerous records of this gift in the Book of Acts.

8. Read Acts 5:12-16. This passage records the spiritual results of physical healings. Summarize the results below.

_____

_____

_____

❐ *Miracles.* This gift of power to do miracles apparently does not include healings since they have already been mentioned as a special gift. These are deeds of supernatural power which alter the normal course of nature. Included would be acts in which God's kingdom is manifested against Satan and his demons.

9. Summarize how the gift of miracles functioned as recorded in Acts 9:36-41.

_____

_____

_____

_____

Overhead
(3 minutes)

Uncover the third main heading and each of its sub-points, as you discuss them, on resource 6B.

❐ *Prophecy.* Prophecy is distinct from revelation, from knowledge, and from doctrine (teaching). Although it may have an effect upon the unbeliever (1 Corinthians 14:24,25), prophecy is primarily for the Church and its members (1 Corinthians 14:4,22). It is a message to others at a specific time to meet a specific need. (See Acts 21:8-11.)

10. Read 1 Corinthians 14:3. What are the primary purposes of prophecy?

_____

_____

_____

❐ *Tongues.* Although the gift of tongues is similar as a manifestation to speaking in tongues as an evidence of the baptism in the Holy Spirit, it is different in purpose. As an evidence, speaking in tongues demonstrates that an individual is being baptized in the Holy Spirit; as a gift, speaking in tongues is for edification of the Church. Not everyone has the gift of tongues, just as all do not have the gifts of healings or of faith.

❏ *The Interpretation Of Tongues.* This gift is necessary to the gift of tongues. It enables what has been said in a tongue to be understood by the entire Church, so all can profit from what has been said in the tongue.

✎ **11. Read 1 Corinthians 14:6,13. What responsibility for using the gift of tongues does Paul give in these verses?**

_____

Read 1 Corinthians 14:12,16,17. Why is this responsibility necessary? _____

_____

Response
(2 minutes)
Have group members share their responses to study guide item 11.

THE USE OF THE GIFTS

Misuse of spiritual gifts has frequently caused needless reproach. The problem, which still exists today among some sincere people, plagued the Corinthian church. We can learn much by taking heed to the principles God has given to govern the use of the gifts of the Spirit.

✓ *The gifts should be used intelligently.* God expects us to be wise in the exercise of the gifts (1 Corinthians 12:1; 14:20). He wants us to grow up in our thinking.

✎ **12. Read 1 Corinthians 14:32. What is being said here about exercising wisdom in regard to the use of spiritual gifts?**

_____

_____

_____

_____

Lecture
(5 minutes)
Use the material in the parallel column to guide the group in a discussion about the use of the gifts.

✓ *The gifts should be used lovingly.* The gifts should not be used maliciously. There should be no rivalry in their use, for rivalry promotes schisms or divisions in the body of Christ.

✎ **13. Read 1 Corinthians 12:31 to 13:3. What is the "more excellent" way of operating in the spiritual gifts?**

_____

_____

Of what use are the gifts of the Spirit without the above characteristic?

_____

_____

Read 1 Corinthians 12:21-25. How will operating in the gifts of the Spirit in the above fashion fulfill this passage?

_____

_____

_____

Discussion
(4 minutes)
Have individuals share their responses to each portion of study guide item 13.
Ask, "What harm can be done to the body of Christ if spiritual gifts are not used in love?"

✓ *The gifts should be used for the good of all.* Selfishness has no place in the use of the gifts. They should either be used for the common good, or should not be used at all in public. (See 1 Corinthians 14:27,28.)

✓ *The gifts should be used in an orderly manner.* Even in the realm of spiritual gifts God has divine order and a pattern. (See 1 Corinthians 14:33,40.)

✓ *The gifts should be used for edification.* The gifts may be used privately for personal edification.

✎ 14. Read 1 Corinthians 14:12,26. What do these verses instruct about the use of the gifts?

_____

_____

_____

As with anything God places into the hands of people, spiritual gifts can be misused. It is fruitless to try to contend that since spiritual gifts are "spiritual" they are never out of order. The Bible clearly shows that the opposite is true. At Corinth the gift of tongues was badly misused. Apparently the Corinthians indulged in speaking in tongues without interpretation. Although the individual speaking was edified, the church did not benefit because there was no understanding of what was being said (1 Corinthians 14:2-11, 16,17). Correctly used, speaking in tongues in a public assembly should be done in the Spirit and with understanding (verses 14,15).

Further, apparently many of the Corinthians were speaking in tongues at the same time. Such behavior did not profit the church.

✎ 15. Read 1 Corinthians 14:23. What impression might an unbeliever get by witnessing many believers speaking in tongues without interpretation?

_____

_____

What is the danger in this? _____

_____

_____

This does not mean that persons should not speak in tongues at prayer time around the altar, after the preaching is finished. The problem at Corinth was that the preacher had no opportunity to proclaim the gospel of the Lord Jesus Christ. Confusion in the congregation brought about through abuse of the gift of tongues made preaching impossible. Thus the individual who came to church to learn about God could not do so.

There was also an excess of speaking in tongues. To correct this condition, Paul instructed that the number of utterances be limited to two or three (1 Corinthians 14:27).

The gift of prophecy was also being misused. They were all prophesying at the same time and there was a reluctance to give others an opportunity to prophesy. The Corinthians were a zealous, but unwise, congregation.

✎ 16. Read 1 Corinthians 14:29-32. What instructions or limitations, if any, did Paul share with the Corinthians concerning using the gift of prophecy?

_____

_____

_____

_____

_____

⇄ **Discussion**
(4 minutes)

Have group members share their responses to study guide item 15.

Ask if anyone has ever been in a service when there was disorderly use of the gifts of the Spirit. If anyone has, have him or her share the experience and any effect it might have had on unbelievers who were also present.

✎ 17. Read 1 Corinthians 14:39,40. What exhortation did Paul leave with the Corinthians regarding spiritual gifts?

_____

_____

Response
(2 minutes)
Have a volunteer share his or her response to study guide item 17.

After his corrections, Paul made certain they were not intimidated in the use of their gifts. A person who utterly neglects spiritual gifts is no wiser than the person who abuses them.

THE VALUE OF THE GIFTS

The gifts of the Spirit are extremely important for the spiritual life of the Church. All the spiritual gifts are valuable and are God's provision for the Church.

✎ 18. Read 1 Corinthians 12:31 and 14:1. What encouragement does Paul give the members of the Corinthian church?

_____

_____

Paul was aware of the value of the gifts. This does not mean all gifts are equally valuable at the same time. Indeed, some of the gifts may be out of place in certain situations and precisely right in others.

✎ 19. Read 1 Corinthians 14:1-5,18. How does Paul indicate the difference in value of some of the gifts?

_____

_____

_____

What seems to be his reasoning for this valuation? _____

_____

_____

Response
(4 minutes)
Have group members discuss their responses to study guide item 19.

SUMMARY

The Church should possess the gifts of the Spirit. By the gifts, God comes directly upon the scene in a church service, encourages or warns, and edifies in a unique way. However, the gifts are to be used in the right way, that is, intelligently, lovingly, for the good of all, in an orderly manner, and for edification. The gifts have been given to us for the building up of the body of Christ.

The gifts which the Spirit gives, through which the Lord ministers, and through which the Father operates, are too valuable, too precious to be misused. With so many warnings against misuse, how can a person know whether or not he or she is moving in God's will when feeling compelled to exercise a spiritual gift? If that individual honestly endeavors to use his or her gift within the guidelines of love, intelligence, order, and edification for the good of all, he or she will not misuse that gift.

God desires for us to earnestly seek after spiritual gifts. If we ask God to be used in such a way, He will grant our desire to be used. We should, by faith, expect to receive. As Pentecostal believers, let us use these gifts to build the body of Christ in love.

Summary
(2 minutes)
Encourage group members to actively seek to be used by the Spirit through His gifts. Point out that these gifts were not just for the Early Church, but for the Church during all time. God has given us ways to be more keenly aware of His will for each of us and for the Church as a whole. We will not all be used in the same way. If we will seek to be used by the Spirit in love, God will grant our desires.

Review
(3 minutes)

Select two or three study guide items from the "Let's Review" section to review the material in this study. If comprehension seems lacking, suggest individuals reread the study.

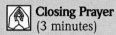 **Closing Prayer**
(3 minutes)

Close the session in prayer, asking God to grant the desires of the hearts of the individuals in this group. Pray that those who wish to be used in the gifts of the Spirit would build their relationship with God, become more aware of His communication with them, and be willing to do what He asks them to do.

Preparing For Next Session

Remind group members to complete study 7 before the next session.

Group Fellowship
(5 minutes)

Encourage everyone to have refreshments and fellowship together before leaving.

LET'S REVIEW

1. What are the five principles that should guide usage of the gifts of the Spirit?

_____

_____

_____

_____

2. Why is it important that we remember God intends the spiritual gifts to be used for the good of all?

_____

_____

_____

_____

3. What are the gifts of the Holy Spirit?

_____

_____

_____

_____

_____

_____

4. What is the purpose of the gift of distinguishing between spirits?

_____

_____

_____

5. What gift(s) are you actively seeking or using?

_____

_____

_____

_____

_____

DIVINE HEALING

Is there any truth to reports of divine healing? Does God still heal people today? Are the healings we hear about merely psychological in nature? Questions such as these are asked by countless people these days as reports of divine healings circulate among believers. To find the answers we again look to the Word of God, for it is our standard of faith and conduct. There we find definite teachings on the matter of divine healing.

As Pentecostals, we believe that God heals today just as He did during Old Testament and New Testament times. It is logical to believe that God, who is able to redeem the immortal souls of humanity, can also heal our mortal bodies. Certainly God who can give spiritual health can also give physical health.

Original sin brought sickness into the world, but healing is available through faith in God.

Study Objective

To understand the origins and reasons for sickness and God's desire to heal the sick and build our faith to receive physical and spiritual healing.

What You Will Need

☐ An overhead projector and blank transparencies or a marker board and appropriate markers.

☐ An overhead transparency of resource 7A, "Why We Get Sick."

☐ Enough copies of resource 7B, "Case Study," for each member of the group.

Getting The Group's Attention

(All times are estimates. 7 minutes)

Write the following statement on an overhead transparency or marker board before group members arrive:

"Miracles of healing were only for the age of the apostles and the first-century church."

When everyone has arrived, have individuals volunteer to respond to the statement. Have them give explanation for their agreement or disagreement, including Scripture references if possible. BE SURE TO KEEP THE DISCUSSION CIVILIZED. It's good for individuals to express their opinions, but be sure they react respectfully to differing opinions.

Transition Statement

The Origin Of Sickness

As we look at divine healing, the first question that comes to mind is, "Why do we get sick?" A simple answer is that a virus, germ, or infection is the cause. But we must look beyond these reasons and consider why people, made by God, are plagued by sickness. Why did God allow sickness to come into His creation? The answer to this question reveals the true cause of sickness.

✎ **1. Read Genesis 2:17 and 3:17,19. What penalty was decreed in these verses?**

_____

_____

Life in the Garden was no longer perfect. Corruption set in, including the corruption of sickness and disease. The death penalty for sin includes physical as well as spiritual death, and sickness often precedes the death to which our corruptible bodies are susceptible. Sometimes sickness happens to us because we exist in mortal bodies.

✎ **2. Read 1 Corinthians 15:54,55. When will sickness no longer be a danger for human beings?**

_____

_____

Sickness is an affliction only here on earth; there will be no sickness in heaven.

Satan And Sickness

Disease and sickness can also be the result of affliction by Satan. When people live in sin, they bring themselves into slavery to Satan, earning for themselves the wages of sin which is death.

✎ **3. Read Romans 6:23 and Ephesians 2:1,2; 4:18. What picture of people living in sin is painted in these verses?**

_____

_____

_____

The sickness which some people experience may be but a precursor to the spiritual death which is theirs because of their sins.

But can Satan attack a believer with sickness and disease? The account of Job is a good example of how Satan, only with God's permission, can afflict a believer with sickness and disease.

✎ **4. Read Job 1:8-10. What is recorded about God's protection of His people against Satan?**

_____

_____

_____

Job was a believer. His testimony was seemingly spotless. God was very pleased and testified to Satan that Job was perfect and upright.

⇄ **Discussion**
(5 minutes)

Have group members share their responses to study guide item 1. Ask, "Since Satan acts as the source of sin and the agent of sickness, does this mean he has powers God does not have?"

Allow 2 or 3 minutes for discussion. Then make this statement, "All the evil in the world today is a result of the Fall. In reality, then, people's willingness to sin is what gives Satan the opportunity to exert an ever-increasing influence for evil in the world, including sickness. Until God totally redeems His creation from the curse of sin, sickness will continue to afflict people. Christians are not immune since we still exist on this planet. But we do have a hope that non-Christians do not have."

Have a volunteer read John 9:1-3. Use this passage to illustrate that sometimes people will have physical ailments. This does not mean that anyone has sinned to cause them.

Have someone share his or her response to study guide item 2.

◩ **Response**
(3 minutes)

Have an individual share his or her response to study guide item 4.

Ask, "Do you think this protection is available to all believers? Why or why not?"

✏ 5. Read Job 1:9-11. What was Satan's opinion of why Job served God?

_____

_____

God knew Job's heart and motives better than Satan so He gave Satan permission to take away all that Job had, but he could not touch Job's physical being. God wanted to demonstrate to Satan that His people did not serve Him only because of His favors.

✏ 6. Read Job 1:13-19. In what ways did Satan afflict Job?

_____

_____

_____

Now read Job 1:20-22. How did Job respond?

_____

_____

_____

Job's reaction frustrated Satan. He presented himself before God once again, and once again God commended Job. Satan then asked for permission to attack Job's body. He was certain that physical affliction would cause Job to turn away from God. So God allowed a physical affliction.

✏ 7. Read Job 2:7-10. After gaining further permission from God to do so, what does Satan do to Job?

_____

_____

Reread verses 9 and 10. How does Job respond to this affliction?

_____

_____

Job's experience vividly demonstrates to us that God protects the believer (Job 1:10), that Satan cannot afflict a believer without God's permission (Job 1:12 and 2:6), and that when sickness or trouble strikes, the believer must remember that God in His love has permitted it (Job 2:10). Those within the hedge of God's protection cannot be touched without God's permission. When God does allow Satan to afflict a Christian, it is always as part of His divine purpose which is being worked out in the believer's life.

✏ 8. Read Job 42:5. What confession concerning his relationship to God does Job make after going through this experience?

_____

_____

God does not allow Satan to afflict Christians on a whim. He always has a purpose. The Christian who is being tested can be assured that all things will work together for good (Romans 8:28). This promise is for all those who love God.

 Discussion
(8 minutes)
Ask group members the following questions:
1. "How does the account of Job warn us about judging people who are going through times of physical affliction? (Is this a negative reflection on their spiritual health?)"
2. "What can we learn from Job's reaction to the loss and suffering dealt to him?" (See study guide items 6-8.)
3. "Why would God remove His hedge of protection from the life of a believer?"
Have a volunteer read Romans 8:28.

Sin And Punishment

Sometimes physical problems are punishments for sin. Just as death entered into the world because of the sin of Adam and Eve, sickness and disease can come upon people because they sin. The Bible contains numerous examples of this principle.

✎ **9. Read Numbers 12:1,2,9,10; 2 Chronicles 21:5,6,18,19; 2 Chronicles 26:3-5,16,19-21; and Acts 12:21-23. Identify on the lines below the four individuals who were punished by God, the affliction each one received, and the sin committed.**

_____

_____

_____

_____

_____

Two of the above individuals were in the custom of living lives that were pleasing to God. In Miriam's circumstance, one instance of rebellion caused her to be stricken with leprosy. Because of Moses' petition to God, her leprosy was a temporary condition. For Uzziah, power and success brought pride. He went so far as to go into the holy place to burn incense, which was an act reserved only for the priests. (See Numbers 18:1-7.) This act was punishable by death. For Uzziah it meant living out his life as a leper in solitude, being unable to ever go into the temple of the Lord again, being stripped of his power, and being buried separately from the other kings, because of his leprosy—the punishment for his sin (2 Chronicles 26:21-23).

But Christ came into the world to eliminate sickness by negating the sin that causes it. His work while on the earth was a preview of the accomplishments of the Cross.

GOD AND HEALING

Some people think that because there are many references to healing in the Old Testament dealing with spiritual health that any mention of healing means deliverance from sin. David was aware of the need for such spiritual healing. He knew that healing for the soul could be found only in God's forgiveness of his sins. So he called out to God for deliverance from the sickness of sin (Psalm 41:4).

Isaiah knew that Israel was afflicted with the sickness of sin and needed healing from God (Isaiah 6:9,10). Matthew's quotation of the passage from Isaiah clearly fixes the responsibility for sin-sickness upon the people (Matthew 13:12,14,15).

Jeremiah saw the need for spiritual healing. In Jeremiah 8:22 he cries out for a balm or a physician that could help Israel. A balm is an ointment with soothing, healing properties. Jeremiah knew that something was needed to restore Israel to spiritual health.

✎ **10. Read Jeremiah 14:19,20; 17:14; and 46:11. What did Jeremiah recognize as the source of Israel's soul sickness?**

_____

What confidence did Jeremiah have for Israel if they would return to God? _____

_____

Whom did Jeremiah know was the only source of spiritual healing? _____

_____

God has provided for our souls the kind of healing that is necessary for sin in the stripes of Christ, if we will turn to Him for it (1 Peter 2:24,25).

Lecture
(2 minutes)

State: "There are many reasons why people get sick. We must be very careful not to judge people who are sick. Unfortunately, some have taught that if a person is sick it is a sure sign that he or she has sinned or is being punished. The examples of Paul (2 Corinthians 12:7-10) and the blind man (John 9:1-3) show us this is not always the case."

Overhead
(4 minutes)

Review the reasons why people get sick by displaying resource 7A, "Why We Get Sick." Have individuals look up the Scriptures given as proofs of some of the reasons.

Small Groups
(6 minutes)

Distribute a copy of resource 7B, "Case Study," to each group member. Have the group break up into smaller groups of four or five and discuss the story and questions given.

Give the groups 4 minutes to discuss among themselves, then have everyone reassemble to the larger group. Ask representatives to share their group's conclusions and allow further group discussion.

Have a few individuals share their responses to study guide item 10.

State: "Both the case study and study guide item 10 demonstrate that the healing of the soul should be our first priority. However, God sometimes does heal someone as a means of reaching the heart."

But is God interested in the physical welfare of individuals?

✎ 11. Read Psalm 103:3 and Jeremiah 17:14. What do these verses say about God's concern for people's well-being?

_____

_____

God made a promise to the Israelites that if they would follow His ways, He would not bring on them any diseases He had brought on the Egyptians, because He was the Lord who heals them (Exodus 15:26). God, who heals the soul, is also able to heal the body.

✎ 12. Read 2 Kings 5:14; 20:1-3,5; Matthew 8:5-13; and Mark 1:32-34. On the lines below list the instances of God's healing recorded in these passages.

_____

_____

_____

In all the recorded incidents of healing in the Bible, God was not a respecter of persons. He healed Jews and Gentiles in both Old and New Testament times.

Most accounts indicate that we should approach Christ with humility and a willingness to do whatever He asks of us.

But the question for now might be, "Does God still heal today?"

The Bible does not place a limit on the power of God to heal. He healed in biblical times; He heals today.

✎ 13. Read James 5:14-16. James gives specific advice in each verse for the person seeking healing. Identify those pieces of advice on the lines below.

_____

_____

_____

A difficult issue for Christians is why God heals some and not others. It is God's nature to heal, and it is promised and practiced throughout the Scriptures. He has not withdrawn His promise. So why is it that many sincere believers do not receive the healing they earnestly pray for? It is important that the suffering believers never let go of their faith that God will heal them and continually affirm their belief that God is their Healer. If the healing never comes, this believer and other Christians must be confident that our Sovereign God is accomplishing higher purposes.

BELIEVERS AND HEALTH

God desires that believers be both spiritually and physically healthy. A spiritually healthy Christian will be concerned about remaining physically healthy. (See 3 John 2.)

✎ 14. Read 1 Corinthians 6:19,20. Why should Christians be concerned about their physical health?

_____

_____

_____

Response
(2 minutes)
Have group members share their responses to study guide item 11.

Discussion
(4 minutes)
Have individuals discuss their responses to study guide item 13. Add to the discussion that it is important we approach God with a sense of humility and a desire to conform to His image.

Have individuals who have received healing from God share testimonies. Also, if individuals know people who have not been healed, encourage them with the information in the paragraph in the parallel column. Sometimes God has a higher purpose we will not know until we reach heaven. It's important to hold firmly to our faith in God.

Response
(2 minutes)
Have group members share their responses to study guide item 14.

A point we should consider is why we want to have good health. The final purpose of life is to glorify God. Health is given to the Christian as a trust which he should keep as a means of carrying out the will of God. Persons who eagerly desire to be healed so they can selfishly pursue their own purposes have forgotten that God is the One to whom they owe their lives.

Another important aspect of divine healing is that we must avoid those things which are sinful or harmful to the body. Even things which are good must be used wisely.

 15. Read Daniel 1:8,12-16; Titus 2:2,3,6,11,12; and 2 Peter 1:5-8. What do these Scripture passages teach us about maintaining a healthy physical body?

_____

_____

_____

What result can we expect if we follow the admonition of these passages?_____

_____

_____

Some activities and foods are not harmful in moderation, but can actually damage the body when carried to excess. The person who fails to get proper rest or take adequate nourishment is also damaging his or her body. Sometimes it is necessary to limit even our work for God. Christians can work too long and at too fast a pace in working for the Lord and bring harm on themselves. Inner conflicts—worry, fear, anger—can drain our physical strength. A sincere surrender of oneself to the will of God and simple daily trust in Him will bring peace, which in turn makes for health of mind and body.

 16. Read Matthew 14:13,22,23; Mark 1:35; 6:31,32,45,46; and Luke 5:15,16; 6:12. What example did Jesus set for us during His time on earth? (List the various ways He took care of himself and His disciples.)

_____

_____

_____

_____

_____

SUMMARY

If one is tempted to say that the day of miracles is past, he or she need only listen to the testimonies of thousands of people who have been healed by the power of God. Tens of thousands have believed the simple passage, "Jesus Christ is the same yesterday and today and forever" (Hebrews 13:8, NIV). They have proof from the Bible that Jesus healed in days past, and as they believe God, they have proof in their own bodies that He still heals today.

Christ's ministry has not changed. While here on earth, He did many good things and healed many people. He desires to do the same today for those who will come to Him in faith. He offers hope for the sick and suffering person.

Christians should live so that they will never have to ask God to heal them for something they could have avoided by living a life of self-control. Spiritual health and physical health often go hand-in-hand. But physical health should not be an indication of Christians' spiritual health. Some could be experiencing the highest compliment of all—God allowing Satan to test them, because He knows they will stand firm in their faith.

Agree/Disagree
(5 minutes)

Have group members share their responses to study guide item 15.

State: "Maintaining our physical bodies as the Bible directs will prevent us from ever getting sick." Have individuals share their reaction to your statement.

(Refer to resource 7A, "Why We Get Sick," to help explain that there are several reasons why people get sick. Sometimes the most healthy person will get sick, and God will use it as a time to develop His relationship with that person.)

Discussion
(3 minutes)

Have group members discuss how following the example of Jesus' activities recorded in study guide item 16 will benefit our spiritual and physical health.

Summary
(2 minutes)

State: "There are two things to remember about healing:

"1. No matter how dramatic a healing may be, healing only postpones the inevitability of death. (See Hebrews 9:27.)

"2. Heaven is the ultimate goal of every Christian, not healing. Christians look forward to a time when there will be no need of healing. (See Revelation 21:4; 22:3.)"

LET'S REVIEW

1. In what two ways is God interested in healing people?

_____

_____

2. Can Satan afflict the believer with sickness and disease? Explain.

_____

_____

_____

_____

3. What was Job's response to the afflictions with which Satan attacked him?

_____

_____

_____

4. What other reasons are there for a believer to have sickness in his or her life?

_____

_____

_____

_____

_____

5. How is spiritual health related to physical health?

_____

_____

_____

_____

6. Is God able to heal today? Support your response with Scripture.

_____

_____

_____

_____

Review
(3 minutes)
Select two or three study guide items from the "Let's Review" section to check the comprehension level of group members. If understanding of the study material seems weak, recommend that individuals work through the study again.

Closing Prayer
(unlimited time)
Pray with any individuals who would like prayer for physical needs of their own or for people they know. Along with the group's prayer of faith for healing, ask God to spiritually strengthen those individuals who have not received healing even though they have prayed for it before.

Preparing For Next Session
Remind group members to complete study 8 before the next session.
Arrange for a group member to give a 3- or 4-minute report on the Passover and the related Feast of Unleavened Bread. Suggest using the following Scriptures: Exodus 12:1-28,43-51; 13:3-10. Also, suggest using a Bible commentary on those passages and a Bible encyclopedia for additional help. Be sure the individual demonstrates the relationship between the Passover and the Lord's Supper.

Group Fellowship
(5 minutes)
Invite individuals to share in fellowship and refreshments before they leave.

Study Objective

To investigate the meaning of the ordinance of Communion and determine to meaningfully partake of the Lord's Supper regularly.

☑ What You Will Need

☐ A group member to give a 3- or 4-minute report on the Passover and the related Feast of Unleavened Bread. (See page 57 for specifics.)
☐ A Bible encyclopedia or standard dictionary.
☐ An overhead projector.
☐ An overhead transparency of resource 8A, "What Is The Lord's Supper?"

▽ Getting The Group's Attention

(All times are estimates. 8 minutes)

Call for the report on the Passover. Allow 2 or 3 minutes for questions and discussion from other group members.

State: "The meaning of the Lord's Supper cannot be separated from its Old Testament background. In 1 Corinthians 5:7 the apostle Paul relates the old and the new by showing Christ to be the passover lamb who was sacrificed for us. The Old Testament celebration was replaced with, or fulfilled by, the New Testament celebration made possible by Jesus' death."

THE LORD'S SUPPER

The cost of redeeming people's souls was colossal. It was nothing less than the blood of Jesus Christ. The sinless One gave up His life for the sinful many.

Just before Jesus was to go to the cross, He had one last meal with His disciples. At this meal He instituted the observance of the new covenant He was about to make available to those who would follow Him. This observance has been labeled the Lord's Supper and the direction to participate in it came straight from Jesus. Christ shared the first Lord's Supper with His closest friends, the disciples, and directed them to continue its observance in remembrance of Him. The Lord's Supper is a memorial to the sacrifice Christ made to obtain eternal salvation for us.

Transition ⇨ Statement

An understanding of the background and significance of the Lord's Supper will help us participate with a proper attitude.

JESUS COMMANDED IT

Several sessions ago, the ordinance of water baptism was studied. As you may recall, an ordinance is a commandment given by Christ which all believers must follow. Most Protestants believe that there are only two such ordinances. The Lord's Supper, or Communion, is the second ordinance.

It was during the last night of His life, the night He was betrayed, that Jesus commanded the observance of the Lord's Supper. When so much was crowding in upon Him, Jesus must have felt the ordinance was very important to have taken the time to set it before His disciples on that last night, just before He went to Gethsemane and to the cross.

✎ **1. Read Luke 22:17-20 and 1 Corinthians 11:23-26. What are the specifics of Jesus' command?**

_____

_____

_____

Until what time are we to continue observing this ordinance? _____

_____

Jesus was aware of the fact that His death was imminent. He had prophesied of it many times during His 3-year time of ministry.

✎ **2. Read Mark 2:20 and John 2:19,21; 6:51. Identify the symbols Jesus used to refer to himself when prophesying of His coming death.**

_____

_____

_____

Unlike us who have no certain knowledge of the future, Jesus knew His ministry would come to an end, He would be betrayed by a friend, and His death would involve great suffering. Jesus, throughout His ministry, had spoken of His death many times. Death to self was central in the mission of Christ. It must also be to us.

In the last few months of His life, Jesus referred to His approaching death even more often. He would share these prophecies while teaching the disciples. While on the way to Jerusalem on His last journey, Jesus prophesied His death with great detail.

✎ **3. Read Luke 18:31-34. What details does Jesus share with His disciples in this passage?**

_____

_____

_____

_____

Read Mark 9:31,32. How had the understanding of the disciples changed since the time of the prophecy recorded in Mark 9 to the prophecy recorded in Luke 18?

_____

_____

Discussion
(2 minutes)
Have individuals discuss the concept of a Church ordinance. (What causes something to be an ordinance?) Use the material in the parallel column to add to the discussion.

Response
(3 minutes)
Have group members share their responses to study guide item 1.

Discussion
(3 minutes)
Have a group member share his or her response to study guide item 2.
Have a volunteer read John 1:29. Ask, "What other title was used to refer to Jesus?"

Once in Jerusalem, during the last week of His life, Jesus shared with His disciples that after the Passover the Son of Man would be betrayed to be crucified. Jesus knew this would be His last Passover. He told the disciples He had been looking forward with great anticipation to sharing this Passover meal with them (Luke 22:15).

4. Read Luke 22:14-16 and 1 Corinthians 5:7. Why, do you think, had Jesus been looking forward to this Passover?

_____

_____

_____

Jesus knew that after this Passover supper, His death was not far off.

Some people have confused the Passover supper and the Lord's Supper, thinking they were the same observance. They were separate events. The Lord's Supper was instituted by Christ after He and His disciples had eaten the Passover supper.

The Passover which they were observing was instituted to commemorate the deliverance of the Israelites from Egypt by the Lord. It reminded them of the Passover lamb whose blood was shed to provide protection for the inhabitants of each house. (See Exodus 12:3-17.) The Lord's Supper which Jesus instituted was to remind Christians of the Lord's death on the cross.

But it is significant that the first Lord's Supper coincided with the Passover.

5. Read John 1:29,36 and 1 Peter 1:18,19. Considering the title used to refer to Jesus in these passages, what is the significance of the timing of the first Lord's Supper?

_____

_____

_____

The night Jesus introduced the Lord's Supper was a night of transition. The Passover, which spoke of God's former covenant with His people, was to be replaced by the Lord's Supper, which celebrates God's new covenant with the sinful people of this world. The event marking the dividing line between the two covenants was the cross of Christ. The death of the Passover lamb provided deliverance from Egypt; the death of Jesus Christ provided deliverance from sin. The one foreshadowed, or pointed toward, the other. When Christ died, the reality symbolized by the Passover observance materialized (Colossians 2:16,17). There was no longer any need for the Passover observance.

THE APOSTLES OBEYED HIM

On the night before He died, Jesus observed the Lord's Supper with His disciples. There was the feeling of close fellowship brought by the ordinance as Jesus once again told the disciples He would become their substitute as He died for their sins.

6. Read Matthew 26:28 and Luke 22:19,20. How did Jesus express to His disciples the message of His substitutionary death?

_____

_____

Christ's death was a once-for-all offering for sin (Hebrews 9:28 and 1 Peter 3:18) much as the sacrifice of the Passover lamb in Egypt. But the observance of the Lord's Supper was never intended to be a one-time-only event carried out by Jesus and His disciples. Rather, it was to be an observance which the apostles—and all Christians to follow—would repeat many, many times. Jesus' words which were translated "this do"

Discussion
(4 minutes)

Have group members share their responses to study guide item 4.

Have a volunteer read Exodus 12:7,13 and Hebrew 9:11-14. Ask, "What is the relevance of the blood in the Passover celebration?"

Response
(3 minutes)

Have several individuals share their responses to study guide item 5.

Brainstorm
(5 minutes)

Ask several individuals to define the term *covenant* in their own words. After the group has listened to a few of these definitions, read the definition from the Bible encyclopedia or dictionary you brought to the session. Ask the group the following questions:

1. "What covenant does the cup represent?"

2. "What was Jesus' part and what is ours?"

Have a volunteer read Hebrews 10:1-4,9,10. Ask, "How is Jesus' sacrifice (the new covenant) better than the old covenant?"

can mean "keep on doing this" (Luke 22:19 and 1 Corinthians 11:24,25). God is aware that we quickly forget. We need a constant reminder of His provision for our sins.

It seems logical that the importance of the ordinance should be equal to the importance of the act it commemorates.

✎ 7. Read 1 Corinthians 11:23. From this text, how would you assume Paul learned about the Lord's Supper?

_____

_____

What does this method of communication say about the importance of this ordinance?

_____

_____

_____

The Lord considers His Supper to be highly important. He revealed to Paul the significance of the Lord's Supper. Paul had been chosen to take the gospel to the Gentiles, kings, and the Children of Israel (Acts 9:15). It was important that he grasped the full significance of the Lord's Supper so that it would be included in his teachings; therefore, God shared it with him.

✎ 8. Read 1 Corinthians 10:16; 11:26. When we take part in the Lord's Supper, what should we recognize about Jesus' death?

_____

_____

What are we saying with our actions when we eat the bread and drink from the cup?

_____

_____

_____

When we partake of the Lord's Supper, we need to remember the great importance God places upon this observance. We should ask God to make it more meaningful to us each time we participate in this ordinance.

THE CHURCH SHOULD CONTINUE TO OBEY HIM

The apostles received the ordinance of the Lord's Supper to pass it on to the Church. Every Christian should observe the ordinance. All believers should be conscious of the meaning of the ordinance of the Lord's Supper as they take part in it.

✎ 9. Read 1 Corinthians 11:20-22. What was the problem in Corinth in regard to the church's observance of the Lord's Supper? Why was this a problem?

_____

_____

_____

_____

Read
(2 minutes)
Have a volunteer read Acts 2:42. Ask, "How does this passage illustrate how seriously the believers took Jesus' and the apostles' teaching?"

Response
(3 minutes)
Have group members share their responses to study guide item 7.
The paragraph in the parallel column immediately following the study guide item might be beneficial to the discussion.

Response
(3 minutes)
Have group members discuss their responses to study guide item 8.

Discussion
(3 minutes)
Have group members share their responses to study guide item 9.
State: "Part of the purpose of the Lord's Supper is to help Christians consider others from Jesus' perspective. The Corinthian church was treating people unequally in their celebration of the Lord's Supper. Believers need to consider their treatment of other people when they examine themselves before taking Communion."

Now read 1 Corinthians 11:30,32,34. What was the result of their abuse? _____

_____

_____

_____

Like anything related to Christianity, this ordinance can be abused. The Corinthian church did not fully understand the symbolism of the bread and the wine. Instead they used it to fulfill their personal appetites. In his letter, Paul gave them, and us, directions for properly observing the Lord's Supper. When properly understood and practiced, the Lord's Supper can become a milestone in the spiritual development of the sincere child of God who desires to obey the command of the Lord.

There are four distinct characteristics relative to the observance of the Lord's Supper.

1. It is a time to remember.

The meaning of the Lord's Supper is the same today as it was in the early days of the Church. When Christians take the Lord's Supper, they are looking back at the way in which Christ died as a substitute for them. The taking of the bread and the cup proclaim that Christ has become their personal Passover Lamb. (See 1 Corinthians 5:7; 11:26.)

In Luke 22:19, Jesus instructed the disciples to observe His Supper in remembrance of Him. In remembrance of what exactly? There are at least a couple things about Christ's life and work for us that we can remember at the time of taking the Lord's Supper.

✎ **10. Read Isaiah 53:4,5 and 2 Corinthians 5:21. In what way do these passages prompt us as we take Communion to remember Christ?**

_____

_____

_____

_____

Now read John 6:48,50,51,53-56. Based on this passage, in what other way should we remember Christ and what He has done for us when we take the Lord's Supper?

_____

_____

_____

When we review the true basis for our salvation—the death of the sinless Lord Jesus Christ for our sins—we can build our Christian character upon that foundation. It is important for us to partake of the Lord's Supper many times in order to remind ourselves again and again that our salvation comes only because of the grace of God. When we adequately remember Christ's death, we see the folly of self-righteousness and spiritual pride. We catch a fresh glimpse of Christ's suffering.

Upon considering His suffering, we also remember what our end would have been had we not met and accepted Christ as our Savior. He is the Bread of Life! His Supper helps us keep that fresh in our minds.

2. It is a time to anticipate.

We are to observe the Lord's Supper until He comes (1 Corinthians 11:26). This speaks of two things: (1) We are to continue observing the event until Jesus returns; and (2) Jesus will come back someday. Jesus' return for His Church is inevitable; we are told to testify of this belief by participating in the Lord's Supper. Each time Christians gather around the Lord's table they remember His words and look forward in anticipation of the

Overhead
(2 minutes)

Display the first main item, "It is a time to remember," of resource 8A, "What Is The Lord's Supper?" and discuss the material in the parallel column related to it.

Overhead
(2 minutes)

Uncover the two subpoints under "It is a time to remember." Have individuals share their responses to study guide item 10 as part of the discussion of these two points.

Overhead
(3 minutes)

Uncover the second main item, "It is a time to anticipate Christ's return," on resource 8A and discuss the related material in the parallel column.

Second Coming. One day the Lord's Supper will be observed for the last time on earth. Then Jesus will return and gather His redeemed children to himself!

3. It is a time to evaluate.

We cannot speak of salvation and the Second Coming without also considering our own selves. The Lord's Supper is a time when a Christian should put himself before the spotlight of the Spirit.

✏️ **11. Read 1 Corinthians 11:27-31. What instructions does Paul give the Corinthians, and us, in this passage? What is the importance of doing this before taking the Lord's Supper?**

_____

_____

_____

_____

_____

As we partake of the ordinance we need to forget our ambitions, plans, and pursuits. We need to evaluate ourselves and our motives in the cold reality of Christ's sufferings for us and His soon coming. We need to place the needs and well-being of others before our own. Then we will see clearly the things that are truly important.

4. It is a time to fellowship.

The word *communion* actually means "fellowship," "partnership," or "sharing." This term appears in 1 Corinthians 10:16 when referring to the cup and the bread which are blessed. When believers take the Lord's Supper, they are drawn into close fellowship with each other as they unite in remembering the shed blood and the broken body that purchased their redemption.

But the fellowship is more than Christian with Christian; it is Christian with Christ. Christians experience the same close fellowship the disciples experienced the night Jesus instituted the ordinance. It's a time when people realize that Jesus has taken their sins, and they share His righteousness. The Lord's Supper seems to be a time when God's presence is especially evident as believers faithfully observe the ordinance of God.

SUMMARY

Jesus has directly given the Church only two ordinances: to be baptized in water, and to remember Him by taking part in Communion or the Lord's Supper. It seems the importance of these two acts is unquestionable since Jesus went out of His way to emphasize them.

Jesus instituted His Supper in recognition of His death to cover the sins of all mankind. It replaced the recognition of the Passover. His sacrifice was a sacrifice once and for all. The Lord's Supper was directed so that Christians throughout time would never forget the substitutionary death of their Lord Jesus Christ. Just as the Passover lamb protected the Israelites in Egypt, Jesus offers protection and redemption for all who believe on Him. His was the greater sacrifice which paid the debt of all humanity in full.

The Lord's Supper is an opportunity for believers to recall the incredible price paid for their redemption. It is an opportunity to identify with Christ in His death (1 Corinthians 10:16). It is an opportunity for believers to realize where they would be without Christ's sacrifice. And it is an opportunity to proclaim that they believe in His return.

Jesus died on our behalf, offering His body and His blood for us. We need to observe the ordinance of the Lord's Supper with a full appreciation of its meaning.

Overhead
(4 minutes)

Uncover the third main point, "It is a time to evaluate our attitude," on resource 8A. Have individuals share their responses to study guide item 11 to enhance discussion of this point.

Have a volunteer read 1 John 1:9 and 5:13. Ask group members the following questions:

1. "To whom is John writing this letter?"

2. "How do John's words in verse 9 tie into the believer's self-examination at the time of the Lord's Supper? Does it mean he or she must be saved all over again?"

Overhead
(4 minutes)

Uncover the last main point, "It is a time to fellowship," on resource 8A. Discuss the "fellowship" aspect of the Lord's Supper as presented in the parallel column. Ask, "Are there dangers in observing the Lord's Supper too often or not often enough? Explain."

State: "The primary objective of observing the Lord's Supper is to be reminded of the work Jesus did on the cross for us. It would seem we should partake as often as it takes for us to continually grasp the reality of His loving sacrifice on our behalf."

Activity
(3 minutes)

Have individuals think of songs that emphasize the blood of Jesus in the redemption of our souls. Select one or two to sing before leaving the session.

LET'S REVIEW

1. Why are water baptism and the Lord's Supper ordinances?

_____

_____

_____

2. When did Jesus command observance of the Lord's Supper?

_____

_____

_____

3. How are the Passover supper and the Lord's Supper different?

_____

_____

_____

_____

4. How did Paul become aware of the ordinance of the Lord's Supper?

_____

_____

_____

_____

5. Explain the four distinct characteristics of the Lord's Supper.

_____

_____

_____

_____

_____

_____

_____

_____

THE CHURCH

W hat is the Church? Is it a building? Is it a group of people? Is it a system of rituals and beliefs? Exactly what or who makes up the Church?

The true foundation of the Church is Jesus Christ himself. A person becomes a member of the Church by faith in the Lord Jesus Christ, not by merely signing the membership roll of a local church. The membership of the Church is far more exclusive than that of church organizations. Many people are united physically with a church group who are not united spiritually with Christ.

Once someone joins the Church through faith in Christ, he or she becomes part of a larger Body. Each member contributes toward the well-being of the entire Body. Every individual needs to recognize his or her function and perform it wholeheartedly for the glory of the Lord, for the good of the Body as a whole, and within the organization of the Church.

Understanding God's design for His Church will help us see we have a part in its operation.

Study Objective

To consider the composition of the true Church and become active in our local church.

What You Will Need

☐ Children's building blocks.
☐ Four volunteers to act out the skit on resource 9A, "There's A Place For All."
☐ Three or four volunteers to sing or play an instrument in the "Harmony" presentation (see page 69).
☐ A marker board or overhead projector with a blank transparency and marker.
☐ A writing instrument for each group member.
☐ A copy of resource 9B, "What Can I Do?" for each group member **AND/OR** a copy of your church's application for membership (see page 71 for details).

Getting The Group's Attention

(All times are estimates. 5 minutes)

Divide the group into two smaller groups. Give each group some building blocks and give them 2 minutes to build a structure using as many of the blocks as possible.

Allow each group to present its structure. Point to a block in the corner or base of each structure. Ask the following questions:

1. "What would happen if you removed that block from your structure or if it was destroyed?"

2. "In light of your response to the first question, why was Jesus the only choice to be the cornerstone and foundation of His Church?"

State: "We all are a part of the Church—each with a specific spot to fill."

Transition Statement

THE FOUNDATION OF THE CHURCH

About 6 months before His death, Jesus asked His disciples a very important question, which is recorded in Matthew 16:13. Jesus asked His disciples who people said He was. The disciples' response to that question indicated the popular opinions people had regarding His identity.

1. Read Matthew 16:13,14. What was the response of the disciples?

_____

_____

What does this say about the clarity of most people's view of Jesus' identity? _____

_____

Jesus wanted to know what opinion His disciples had concerning His identity. Embracing the opinions held by the general public regarding who He was would never work for His purpose. Jesus could never build the Church on the strength of these the public thought He was, even though they were great people of God. So He became more personal regarding His inquiry of the disciples.

2. Read Matthew 16:15,16. How did Peter respond to Jesus' more direct question to the disciples?

_____

_____

Jesus' question to the disciples was important; it was doubly important considering to whom it was directed. They had been with Him, hearing Him teach and seeing Him work. Of all people, they were given the best opportunity to discover His identity.

Peter's answer was a good one, having its source in divine revelation rather than in the opinions of other people. Jesus even commented on the fact it was the Father who had opened Peter's spiritual eyes to recognize who Jesus really was.

Peter's confession of faith revealed a foundation upon which Jesus could build His Church. He could not build it upon the uncertain foundation of men, even men like John the Baptist, Elijah, Jeremiah, or even Peter. At best, these men of God could be stones.

3. Read Matthew 16:17,18. How does Jesus respond to Peter's answer?

_____

_____

In order to understand that Jesus' response was not to imply that Peter would be the foundation of the Church, we must look at the Greek text and how it is literally transliterated into the English text. The word *Peter* is a transliteration of the Greek word *petros*, which means "stone" or "a piece of the rock." The word *rock* is a translation of the Greek word *petra*, which means "solid bedrock." The use of the two distinctly different words shows that Jesus did not intend to build His Church upon Peter. Peter was a stone in the total structure, not the "solid bedrock" upon which the Church stands. Jesus Christ is the foundation.

4. Read Ephesians 2:19,20 and 1 Peter 2:4-8. How do these two passages refer to Jesus?

_____

_____

_____

Response
(5 minutes)
Have group members share their responses to study guide items 1 and 2. Ask the following questions:
1. "Why were the disciples able to see who Christ really was?"
2. "What can we learn from the example of the disciples?"

Discussion
(4 minutes)
Have a volunteer share his or her response to study guide item 3.
Discuss with the group the words *petros* and *petra* as presented in the parallel column and how their translation impacts our interpretation of Scripture concerning the foundation of the Church.

Reread 1 Peter 2:4,5. How does Peter refer to believers? _____

_____

Just as Peter is a stone in the structure of the Church, so are we. He became a stone through his confession of faith (Matthew 16:16). We become stones in the Church in the same way Peter did, that is, through faith or belief in Christ Jesus as the Son of the Living God. Peter knew he and all believers were just parts of the structure of the Church. He knew that Jesus Christ was the Chief Cornerstone.

A cornerstone is a foundation stone occupying a key position in the structure of a building. In biblical times, a cornerstone not only united two walls, but it also bore the pressures exerted by those walls.

✎ **5. Read Isaiah 53:6,12. Considering the previous paragraph's description of a cornerstone, how would the verses in Isaiah describing the coming Messiah point to Jesus?**

_____

_____

_____

Christ took on the sins of all of us so He could reconcile us to God. He is the cornerstone of the foundation laid by the apostles and prophets. Jesus is the Cornerstone who joins the living stones of the Church together.

✎ **6. Read Isaiah 28:16; 1 Corinthians 3:10,11; and Ephesians 2:21,22. What important facts about the Foundation of the Church are shared in these passages?**

_____

_____

_____

_____

Jesus supports our weight and joins believers together. The apostles and prophets presented Him as the Cornerstone as they shared the gospel. Jesus is not only the cornerstone of the Church; He was also the cornerstone of the witness presented by the apostles and prophets.

THE MEMBERSHIP OF THE CHURCH

The Bible presents several word pictures of the Church. We have just seen it described as a building of which Christ is the foundation and chief cornerstone. The Church is also pictured as the Body of which Jesus is the head—the spiritual body of Christ.

Christians are not only pictured as individual living stones composing a building; they are also pictured as individual parts composing a body.

Although no one picture fully embraces the complete glory and majesty of the Church, each helps us visualize the invisible Church. Each picture gives us an intimate glimpse into the close relationship which Christ has with each member of His Church.

✎ **7. Read Ephesians 1:22,23 and Colossians 1:18. By whose authority and for what purpose is Christ the Head of the Church?**

_____

_____

_____

▨ Response
(2 minutes)
Have group members share their responses to study guide item 5.

⇄ Discussion
(5 minutes)
Have a few individuals share their responses to study guide item 6. Ask the following questions:
1. "How can we be sure to follow Paul's example in 1 Corinthians 3:10?"
2. "What harm comes from laying a poor foundation when constructing a building?"
3. "How does this concept relate to the building of the Church of Christ?"

⊥ Lecture
(2 minutes)
Describe the analogy of the Church being the body of Christ using the material in the parallel column. Include in the discussion your response to study guide item 7. Allow other group members to add to the discussion.

Read Ephesians 5:23,24. How should we honor Christ as the Head of the Body?

_____

✎ 8. Read 1 Corinthians 12:13 and Ephesians 5:23. How do people become members of the Church?

_____

_____

_____

    The Church is composed of all those who have accepted Christ as Savior. Just as being registered on the membership roll of a local church does not make someone a part of the Church, not being registered does not exclude someone from membership in the Church. As long as that person believes on Christ, he or she is a member of the body of Christ, the Church.

    Every member of the body of Christ is important. The well-being and proper functioning of the Body is dependent upon the well-being and proper functioning of all the members of the Body. Paul shares this principle with some humorous words.

✎ 9. Read 1 Corinthians 12:12,14-17,19-26. In what ways does Paul compare the functioning of the body of the Church to a human body's functions?

_____

_____

_____

_____

What does Paul say about the status of the different body parts? _____

_____

_____

_____

_____

What is the purpose of maintaining this status? _____

_____

_____

✎ 10. Read 1 Corinthians 12:18 and Ephesians 4:16. Who determines where each member of the Body fits?

_____

What is necessary for the Body to benefit (grow)? _____

_____

_____

    Proper functioning of the Body means that every member of the Body is in its right place performing its proper task. Paul highlights this in his comical discussion of the different body parts and their jealousy of other body parts (1 Corinthians 12:15-17).

Response
(4 minutes)
    Have a volunteer read the Scripture reference from study guide item 9. Then have individuals share their responses to study guide item 9.

Presentation
(4 minutes)
    Introduce the participants (their character names) in the skit. When the skit is completed, ask group members what they would do without one of their seemingly unimportant body parts (e.g., big toe, eye lashes, thumb, etc.).

Discussion
(4 minutes)
    Have group members share their responses to study guide item 10. Ask, "Why is it important to remember who assigns our position within the Church regardless of whether we have highly visible or behind-the-scenes positions?"

The place each member of the body of Christ occupies in that Body is dependent upon God and His will, and is not dependent upon the ambitions or desires of each individual. Each member is assigned to the position and function in which he or she can best work for the general welfare of the Body. Each Christian can know that God, in His love and mercy, has placed him or her in the best possible ministry. That is why, for example, the Holy Spirit has bestowed different spiritual gifts upon different members of the Church (1 Corinthians 12:8-11). God knows through which members of the Church He can best exercise specific gifts for the good of all the members of the Body.

✏ **11. Read Romans 12:4-8. In what manner should members fulfill the demands of their different positions and functions?**

_____

_____

_____

✏ **12. Read 1 Peter 4:10,11. What is the ultimate purpose of members properly filling their positions?**

_____

_____

As we trust God in His assignment of responsibility within the Body and begin to operate in those assigned functions to the best of our ability, personal glory will diminish. God is glorified when each of us functions as a good steward of the particular position given to us. Even if a job or position seems quite routine, it is eternally important because it is the job God has assigned.

No member of the Church should feel that his or her ministry, service, or gift makes him or her better than some other member. It is God who is supposed to be glorified by the Church, not the members of the Church. God does not view the functioning of one member of the Body as being more honorable than that of another. (See 1 Corinthians 12:24-26.)

✏ **13. Read Romans 12:3 and Philippians 2:3-11. How should we treat one another?**

_____

_____

_____

_____

After whom are we to fashion our attitude toward others? _____

THE ORGANIZATION OF THE CHURCH

The Church, the body of Christ, is a living thing—an organism. Every part of that organism, every member, is equal to every other part or member. The head of the Church is Christ. Every other member is subject to Him.

However, every body is assembled in a certain way. For example, as we examine our own bodies, we see that they are put together in a specific way. The way a body is put together is called its organization. No body exists without some degree of organization. When a body loses control of its arms and legs, it is partially impaired. It cannot perform its tasks perfectly, as originally designed. Likewise, the body of Christ must be a smooth-working organism that proceeds in an organized manner.

In the Early Church the need for organization came as the scope of the Church enlarged. The Church was centered in Jerusalem, and the apostles were the leaders or overseers of that Church.

Response
(2 minutes)
Have group members share their responses to study guide item 14.

14. Read Acts 1:15-17,20-26 and 6:1-7. For what two reasons did the leaders of the Church have to make changes in the organization of the Early Church?

_____

_____

_____

_____

As more local churches came into being, they each had their own bishop, or overseer, and deacons (Philippians 1:1). These bishops and deacons exercised important ministries in the Early Church.

Bishops (overseers):

Our word *bishop* means "overseer," which is a good translation of the Greek word *episkopos* from which it comes. The function of bishops was to oversee a local church. They were also called *elders* or *shepherds*. They were responsible for the spiritual condition of the local church. Most people today would call them *pastors*.

15. Read Acts 20:28. Who did Paul say had placed these men over the local churches?

_____

In present time, when a pastor comes to lead a congregation, the members should consider that the Holy Spirit has appointed this person for their church for that particular period. Many churches could have greater influence for the Lord if other members of the Body would accept their pastor as selected by God.

16. Read 1 Timothy 3:1-7; 5:17-19; and Titus 1:5-9. How should overseers or pastors be treated?

_____

_____

What are the qualifications for holding the position of overseer? _____

_____

_____

_____

_____

_____

_____

_____

_____

Discussion
(4 minutes)
Have group members share their responses to study guide item 16. On a marker board or overhead transparency, list the qualifications for the position of overseer or pastor. Leave room next to this list to list the qualifications for deacons later in the session.

Deacons:

The office of deacon is also highly spoken of in the Bible. Our word *deacon* comes from the Greek word *diakonos*, which we have borrowed and made part of our language. The Greek word is translated to reference the work of a servant, but not a slave.

17. Read Acts 6:1-4. What incident prompted the selection of the original deacons?

_____

_____

What did the work of the deacons free the apostles to do? _____

_____

Now read 1 Timothy 3:8-13. What are the qualifications for serving as a deacon?

_____

_____

_____

_____

Deacons were added to free those exercising the pastoral ministry from the cares of the temporal affairs of the church. The original deacons were selected to "wait on tables" (NIV) or "serve tables" (KJV). The word *tables* in this passage (Acts 6:2) actually refers to money tables. Therefore, deacons were most likely responsible for the financial affairs of the church. This allowed the apostles more time for preaching and praying. The appointment of deacons should not imply that one job was more important than the other, since we have already learned that all members of the Body are vital and important (1 Corinthians 12:15-17). What this does show is that temporal affairs of the church must be tended to. Christ expects His Church to meet both its temporal and spiritual responsibilities.

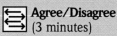 **18. Read Acts 11:1-18; 11:27-30; 15:1-30 (especially vv. 6,12,25). From these passages, how were the individual churches of the Early Church associated? (Was there an overriding governing body?)**

_____

_____

_____

The form of government demonstrated by the Early Church assemblies is called "congregationalism." It allows flexibility to meet changing needs and conditions. There was a close fellowship which existed among the churches of that time. Bound together by their mutual love for Christ and one another, they were careful to help each other in times of need, to receive missionaries and evangelists who were referred by another assembly, and to proclaim the good news of the gospel of Jesus Christ.

SUMMARY

First and foremost, we must believe that Jesus Christ is the foundation of the Church. No one else is able to fulfill this function. Every believer is a part of His Church, but Jesus is the One who holds it together.

God has given each believer a gift to be used for the good of the Church and to the glory of God. As all believers work together in harmony and love, the Church will benefit and will grow. God's perspective is that every member of the body of Christ is equally important and all should work as servants to the others.

God has also built a system of government for local churches. He establishes pastors and provides deacons and other lay leadership to care for both the spiritual and temporal aspects of church responsibility. And in all of this, a believer's goal should be to love others and work toward sharing the good news of Jesus Christ with the world.

Discussion
(5 minutes)

Have group members share their responses to study guide item 17. List the qualifications for deacons next to the list of qualifications for pastors.

Ask the following questions:

1. "Do pastors and deacons serve the same functions today as they did in New Testament times? Why or why not?"

2. "Why are the qualifications for these two positions so strict?"

Agree/Disagree
(3 minutes)

Have group members respond to the following statement: "Being a deacon excludes people from other forms of preaching or evangelism ministry."

Have different volunteers read Acts 6:5; Acts 7:2,51-55, 59,60; and Acts 8:4,5,26-35. These passages show that both Stephen and Philip were also used in ways other than the traditional role of deacon.

Activity
(3 minutes)

Distribute a copy of resource 9B, "What Can I Do?" and/or a copy of your church's application for membership to each individual. Distribute writing instruments to individuals if needed. Give them time to look over the handouts and complete them if they would like. Collect them afterwards to pass on to your pastor or church administrator, or have individuals give the handouts to your pastor personally.

NOTE: Resource 9B is not to be a comprehensive listing of opportunities for service in the local church. Feel free to add any area of service your church may have that is not included. Also, ask your pastor for approval to use this handout before distributing it to group members.

Review
(3 minutes)

Select two or three study guide items from the "Let's Review" section to check the comprehension level of group members. If understanding of the study material seems weak, recommend that individuals work through the study again.

Closing Prayer
(2 minutes)

Pray that God would help group members find their place in the Body and do their best to fulfill that position for the glory of God.

Preparing For Next Session

Remind group members to complete study 10 before the next session.

Group Fellowship
(5 minutes)

Invite individuals to share in fellowship and refreshments before they leave.

1. Who did the general public believe Jesus was? How about the disciples?

_____

_____

_____

2. Describe a cornerstone.

_____

_____

_____

_____

3. How does Jesus fulfill the description as the cornerstone of the Church?

_____

_____

_____

_____

4. How do people become members of the Church?

_____

_____

_____

5. What was the function of deacons in the Early Church?

_____

_____

_____

_____

6. What was the function of bishops (overseers) in the Early Church?

_____

_____

_____

_____

STEWARDSHIP

Every Christian is a steward of God, accountable to Him for that stewardship. So what does it mean to be a Christian steward? Basically, it means Christians are managers of the earthly goods which God has committed to their care. They are responsible for the way they use those things entrusted to them.

This stewardship is based on two fundamental facts: (1) Everything a believer possesses comes from God; and (2) Everything a believer has should be consecrated or dedicated to God. Christians are to be good stewards of God's money, time, energy, health—everything they have or possess.

When tithing, it is important that we do not think we are giving God a part of what we earn. We must remember that we only have what God gives us. A better view is to realize that we are actually keeping 90 percent of His money for ourselves.

God has provided guidelines to becoming faithful stewards.

Study Objective
To examine the biblical concept of stewardship and become more faithful stewards.

What You Will Need
☐ Paper and a writing instrument for each group member.
☐ A marker board or overhead projector with blank transparencies and markers.
☐ A transparency of resource 10A, "Examples Of Faithful Stewardship."
☐ Enough copies of resource 10B, "Who Would Want To Do Less?" for each individual.

Getting The Group's Attention
(All times are estimates. 5 minutes)
Distribute the paper and writing instruments to group members as they arrive. Have them write out what they think of when they hear the term *stewardship*.

Have volunteers share their responses. Write them on a marker board or overhead transparency as they are shared. A large percentage of the responses will probably involve money or financial matters.

Ask, "Does stewardship only involve money? Why or why not?"

State: "If everything we have is from God, that would include time, health, and spiritual blessings, as well as money. God asks us to use *all* things wisely."

Transition Statement

THE SOURCE OF STEWARDSHIP

What is a steward? The Greek word we translate *steward* actually means "manager of a household." During the time of the Early Church, stewards managed the property of other individuals.

✎ **1. Read Luke 12:42 and 16:1,2. How does one become a steward?**

_____

How long does one remain a steward? _____

_____

How can these two concepts be applied to Christian stewardship? _____

_____

_____

_____

God is the source of Christian stewardship. Christians must remember that everything they have comes from God. He is the source of all that a Christian possesses.

It is important for believers to remember from where they receive all they have. That doesn't always happen. People begin to see their own hard work and efforts as the source of their income and wealth. This forgetfulness has often been evident in God's people, in the Old Testament, the New Testament, and today.

✎ **2. Read Deuteronomy 8:10-12,17,18. What warning and then reminder does God give the Israelites in this passage?**

_____

_____

_____

What does God cite as the reason for His reminder (vv. 12-14)? _____

_____

_____

Israel failed to heed God's warning and was punished for it. She did not recognize that God was the source of all that she had.

✎ **3. Read Hosea 2:5,8,9,12. How did God punish Israel for her unfaithfulness?**

_____

_____

_____

What justification did He give for this punishment? _____

_____

In the New Testament, Jesus told a parable about a rich man who forgot that his wealth came from God (Luke 12:16-21). This man refused to consider himself as a steward of God.

Brainstorm
(5 minutes)
Have group members share their responses to study guide item 1. Discuss how we can become good stewards. As they are mentioned, have a volunteer write responses on a marker board or overhead transparency.

Response
(4 minutes)
Have individuals share their responses to study guide items 2 and 3.
Ask, "According to these accounts, who is responsible for meeting our needs?"

✎ 4. Read Luke 12:16-19. What is evident about this man's opinion of himself?

_____

_____

Read Luke 12:20,21. What is God's reaction to the rich man's plans? _____

_____

_____

How could the rich man have avoided this punishment? _____

_____

_____

The rich man had forgotten God. He gave himself credit for his own prosperity, when in reality, God owned everything he had, even his life. In telling this story, Christ was warning against the sins of ingratitude, self-centeredness, and greed. Believers shouldn't get so caught up in material prosperity that they lose sight of the source of that wealth. We must remember we serve a jealous God (Exodus 20:5) who desires and demands that we honor Him with obedience to His commands. When we forget to acknowledge His provision for us, we disobey Him and display love and honor to something else. We must remember we are God's stewards.

THE RESPONSIBILITIES OF STEWARDSHIP

A steward has an obligation to the one who appointed him or her. The apostle Paul wrote to the Corinthian believers concerning the requirement of their stewardship.

✎ 5. Read 1 Corinthians 4:1,2. What is required of stewards?

_____

God's standards are often different from those people establish. He wants stewards who are faithful in the use of the goods which have been committed to their care. We often want people who are talented, brilliant, and witty. But God wants individuals who, regardless of their abilities, put these talents to consistent, faithful use.

In Paul's second letter to the Corinthians, he was able to point to some Christians who had been faithful stewards—the Macedonians.

✎ 6. Read 2 Corinthians 8:1-5. What was the economic status of the Macedonians?

_____

Identify the areas, in their giving, for which Paul commended the Macedonians.

_____

_____

_____

_____

Why is it the most liberal givers are often those who have the least?

The Macedonians were rich in their generosity toward others. They gave because they and all they possessed were already committed to God. God not only owned their

⇄ **Discussion**
(2 minutes)
Ask the following questions:
1. "Consider the account of the rich man recorded in Luke 12:16-21. To what extent is God the giver of all things?"
2. "How does tithing help us remember the Source of our possessions?"

◩ **Response**
(4 minutes)
Have group members share their responses to study guide items 5 and 6.

▱ **Overhead**
(2 minutes)
Display the first line of resource 10A, "Examples Of Faithful Stewardship."
Discuss the faithful stewardship demonstrated by the Macedonians using the material following study guide item 6 in the parallel column.

possessions; He owned them. We do not have to possess great wealth to be great stewards of God's goods. We merely have to be faithful with what He gives us.

✎ **7. Read Luke 21:1-4. How did Jesus use the account of the poor widow to demonstrate faithfulness in stewardship?**

_____

_____

_____

Jesus was a faithful steward also. His life is an example for us to follow. He gave up far more than any human could ever be expected to relinquish when He came from heaven to earth to redeem us from sin.

✎ **8. Read John 17:5; 2 Corinthians 8:9; and Philippians 2:5-8. What were the things Jesus gave up so that we could be saved?**

_____

_____

_____

_____

Considering the magnitude of what Christ gave up, how can Christians refuse to give up the little we have?

God expects Christians to be faithful to the responsibilities of our stewardship. He wants us to use the earthly treasures which He has committed to our care to provide for our eternal future. It seems that too many people live beyond their incomes in order to look good to those around them. Easy credit facilitates this trend and people get in over their heads. Does it seem right when some Christians say they can't pay their tithes and it's because they have overextended themselves and spent their money elsewhere? Does poor decision-making justify robbing from God (Malachi 3:9)?

It's all too easy to get caught up in this whirlwind. Most of our generation has grown up with not only enough, but more than enough. It takes strong Christian character to keep our balance. We need to be careful not to judge them, but to try to guide.

✎ **9. Read Matthew 6:24-34. What does Jesus say about loving God and money?**

_____

_____

What assurance does Christ give us concerning our care? _____

_____

_____

What should be our first priority in life? Why? _____

_____

_____

_____

Overhead
(2 minutes)
Uncover the second item on resource 10A. Briefly review the faithfulness of the poor widow as related in Luke 21:1-4.

Handout
(6 minutes)
First uncover the third item on resource 10A.

Then distribute a copy of resource 10B, "Who Would Want To Do Less?" to each individual. Give group members 4 minutes to complete the work sheet. Urge them to carefully consider each question and answer honestly.

After 4 minutes, ask them if the work sheet illuminated any areas where they could improve their stewardship.

State: "Hold on to this work sheet and use it as a stepping stone, not a weight. If you see an area where you need to improve, just begin working at it. God will honor your faithfulness."

Discussion
(4 minutes)
Have group members share their responses to study guide item 9.

Ask, "Since God tells us not to love money, does that mean He wants Christians to be poor? Why or why not?"

As Christians we must keep the right balance between legitimate ambition and spiritual dedication. We must make money our servant; never our master. We should see our blessings as more opportunities to bless others for God's kingdom.

Some Christians don't pay tithes (one-tenth of their income) because they think tithing is legalistic. While God did establish His design for stewardship in the Mosaic law, it was practiced before the Law was given.

10. Read Genesis 14:18-20 and Hebrews 7:1,2. What account is related in these Scripture passages and who were the parties involved?

_____

_____

_____

_____

11. Read Genesis 28:20-22. In the statement of his vow, how did Jacob demonstrate understanding of stewardship to God?

_____

_____

_____

Both of these men demonstrated faithful stewardship of what God had given them, before the Law was even recorded. When Jesus came, He gave an exhortation concerning tithing, using as example the legalistic Pharisees themselves.

12. Read Matthew 5:20 and 23:23. How did Jesus emphasize the importance of tithing in the Matthew 5:20 reference?

_____

_____

_____

_____

Under the Law, tithing was required; under grace, surely people will not want to give less to the Lord. Tithing, under grace, is a minimum.

13. Read 1 Corinthians 16:2; 2 Corinthians 8:7,8,10-12; 9:7. Paul gives several instructions to the Corinthian Christians regarding their giving. On the lines below list these guidelines.

_____

_____

_____

_____

_____

As God gives, the believer should give back to God. Every Christian should remember that he or she cannot outgive God. And we can't use the excuse that we don't make enough to tithe. God holds us responsible for what we have, not for what we don't have. God expects us to be faithful in our giving as well as to give with the proper attitude.

Overhead
(4 minute)

Uncover the fourth and fifth items on resource 10A. Have group members share their responses to study guide items 10 and 11 as a way of discussing these stewards.

Discussion
(2 minutes)

Have group members share their responses to study guide item 12.

Ask, "Do you think Jesus was using the Pharisees as a positive example of stewardship? Why or why not?"

State: "Even though the Pharisees tithed, their motivation for doing so was strictly legalistic. It appears they were not concerned about the true reason for doing so; they just did it because the Law demanded it."

Response
(3 minutes)

Have group members share their responses to study guide item 13. Have a volunteer record responses on a marker board or an overhead transparency as they are shared.

THE RESULTS OF STEWARDSHIP

"What's in it for me?" is not the proper attitude for giving to the Lord for the accomplishment of His work. God has promised, however, He will give certain things to those who are faithful stewards.

Blessing

God has promised to give back to those who give to Him. The blessing is both physical and spiritual.

14. Read 2 Corinthians 9:6,8,10,11. What does this passage say about receiving physical blessing from God as a result of our giving?

_____

_____

_____

For what purpose does He bless us? _____

_____

As great as the physical blessing may be, the spiritual blessings that come as the result of faithful giving are far greater.

15. Read 2 Corinthians 9:12-14. What spiritual blessings result from faithful giving?

_____

_____

_____

We don't always know exactly how our giving is used in the kingdom of God. Someone might hear the message of Jesus Christ; someone else might benefit from a new coat or pair of shoes. According to Paul, these individuals don't necessarily know who financed the gifts they received, but they thank God and also pray for that anonymous person. Thus, God will be glorified.

Fellowship

Good stewardship is also a form of fellowship. *Webster's Collegiate Dictionary, Tenth Edition* defines *fellowship* as a "community of interest, activity, feeling, or experience." Another way of stating this could be "people sharing in an interest, activity, feeling, or experience."

16. Read 2 Corinthians 8:4 and Philippians 1:7. How did Paul refer to the giving of the Macedonian churches?

_____

_____

How is this a form of fellowship? _____

_____

_____

Selfishness cuts us off from a fellowship which is ours when we assume our proper part in bearing the load of ministry. When we are willing to participate with other

---

▨ Response
(3 minutes)
Have group members share their responses to study guide items 14 and 15.

▨ Response
(2 minutes)
Have group members discuss their responses to study guide item 16.

Christians in a common goal through giving, we create an opportunity for fellowship with them.

Service

Not every Christian can preach, lead singing, teach the Bible, or conduct a formal worship service. But every Christian can join in the form of Christian service which stewardship provides. Christians who work all week in careers outside the church can transform some of the hours of that week into service for Christ by giving money earned to the work of the Lord Jesus Christ. God has provided all believers this opportunity for service.

Testimony

Good stewardship is one of the best and most genuine ways a Christian can testify of his or her love for Christ. Words are cheap, but when backed with a generous love gift, there is a ring of sincerity to one's testimony. On the other hand, people who speak often of their great love for Christ but fail to assume their responsibility as a steward of Christ, demonstrate a lack of genuine interest in Christ's work.

 17. Read Matthew 10:8 and Luke 6:38. What do these passages admonish us to do?

_____

What should be our motivation? _____

What will be the result?_____

Cheerful giving is a witness that grace has been received from God. All Christians should be good givers, within their means. Giving is an enriching experience.

The stingy individual often finds instead of having more, he or she has less. As stated earlier in this study, we can't outgive God. Many believers can attest to this fact; it has been proven again and again. But neither should we give expecting God to give back. If we take stewardship back to its most basic level, we see it is all tied to our motivation.

 18. Read 1 Samuel 16:7, 1 Chronicles 28:9, Psalm 44:21, Luke 16:15, and 1 Corinthians 4:5. What do these verses tell us about how God judges us and our actions?

_____

_____

Only God and each individual know the condition and attitude of his or her heart. As we give, let's remember what we have already received from God and not think about what we might get in return. When we are thankful for what we've been given, we will have a greater desire to give to someone else.

SUMMARY

Stewardship is not an option. It is a command and a necessity. True spirituality and financial giving have always gone hand-in-hand. The handling of money is the acid test of character. Some Christians who have done well in other areas have failed in this one.

Doing anything worthwhile in life takes determination. Tithing takes a lot of it. People who have never practiced tithing may grow panicky at the thought of giving away one-tenth of their income before spending any on themselves. They may look at bills and say, "I can't get along with nine-tenths! I need ten-tenths, and even more." But multitudes of tithers could rise up and testify that God has a miraculous way of making the nine-tenths go farther than the ten-tenths.

More self-discipline is probably required in the management of money than any other realm. It takes real determination to take out the Lord's tenth every payday before making any personal expenditures. And remember, God loves a cheerful giver. Just stop and think about all He has given you. That ought to help your attitude!

Lecture
(2 minutes)
Discuss the topic of "Service" as presented in the parallel column. Point out that for some people, giving is a spiritual gift from God. Have someone read Romans 12:6-8.
State: "This does not relieve anyone from the responsibility of giving. We have all received everything we have from God, therefore we all need to recognize that fact through giving."

Response
(4 minutes)
Have group members share their responses to study guide items 17 and 18. Ask in a rhetorical fashion, "What does your attitude toward Christian stewardship say about your relationship with God?"

Summary
(3 minutes)
State: "Becoming a faithful steward requires determination and consistent stewardship practice, such as tithing and giving of offerings. We each need to review resource 10B, 'Who Would Want To Do Less?' and determine any areas we want to work on in our effort to become more faithful stewards of what God has given us."

Review
(3 minutes)

Select two or three study guide items from the "Let's Review" section to review the material in this study. If comprehension seems lacking, suggest individuals reread the study.

 Closing Prayer
(2 minutes)

Close with prayer, asking God to help each group member honestly evaluate his or her level of stewardship and be willing to follow more closely the guidelines God has established.

 Discussion
(5 minutes)

Have group members begin to think about topics they would like to study upon completion of *Biblical Foundations*. You may wish to consider another title from the *Spiritual Discovery Series*. Information about additional titles may be obtained from your *Radiant Life* distributor.

 Preparing For Next Session

Remind group members to complete study 11 before the next session.

Obtain a list of the missionaries your church supports and any available missionary newsletters your church may have on file.

 Group Fellowship
(5 minutes)

Encourage everyone to have refreshments and fellowship together before leaving.

LET'S REVIEW

1. What is a steward?

_____

_____

_____

2. What is the source (the basis) of Christian stewardship?

_____

_____

3. What characteristic must a steward have? Whom did Jesus use as an example of this?

_____

_____

_____

_____

4. In 1 Corinthians 16 and 2 Corinthians 8 and 9, what instructions did Paul give regarding giving?

_____

_____

_____

_____

_____

5. What results come from faithful giving?

_____

_____

_____

_____

STUDY 11

MISSIONS

Originally, everyone on earth knew about God, but gradually people deliberately turned away from their Creator. When this began to happen, each succeeding generation knew less about God than the generation which preceded it. Only effective missionary work throughout the world can restore the knowledge of God to those who have lost it.

When we talk about the world being the mission field, we must not neglect our own country. Missions involves both foreign and home ministries. We can support both arms of missions financially and through prayer. The important thing is that we do support missions.

We all are not called to give our lives entirely over to active missionary work. But in one sense, all Christians are missionaries, for a missionary is a person sent out with the job of preaching or sharing the gospel of the Lord Jesus Christ. Each one of us is a missionary where we work, to our neighbors, to our families, and to our friends. We are all a part of God's missions plan.

Jesus' command to preach to all the world demands a response from Christians.

Study Objective

To study the biblical command for missions and respond to that call.

What You Will Need

☐ Paper and a writing instrument for each individual.
☐ An overhead projector and blank transparency or marker board and appropriate marker.
☐ Copies of resources 11A, "Bapa's Quest," and 11B, "The Partnership Of Missions."
☐ A list of the missionaries and missionary efforts your church supports and any available newsletters.

Getting The Group's Attention

(All times are estimates. 8 minutes)

Distribute paper and a writing instrument to each group member. Divide the group into two smaller groups.

Have members of one group write their responses to a person who says, "The world isn't so bad. Missionaries try to change the culture of people and that brings worse problems."

Have members of the other group write their responses to this statement: "People are not responsible to God if they have never heard the gospel." (See Romans 1:18-23.)

Give the groups 5 minutes to write their responses and then formulate a response which reflects, as closely as possible, the attitude of the whole group. Allow 3 minutes for them to share their responses and engage in discussion. Ask, "How does our response to these questions affect our response to the missions command of Jesus?"

Transition Statement

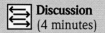 **Discussion**
(4 minutes)

Ask, "What does missions and being a missionary mean to you?" Allow several to respond and write their responses on a marker board or blank overhead transparency.

Discuss briefly the material in the parallel column concerning the definition of a missionary.

 Response
(2 minutes)

Have group members share their responses to study guide item 1.

 Handout
(3 minutes)

Have a volunteer read Romans 1:20. Distribute resource 11A, "Bapa's Quest," to the group members and have them read it.

Ask the following:

1. "Does this story reinforce the idea that missionaries are not really needed? Why or why not?"

2. "In what ways did Bapa Timmy fulfill the role of missionary?"

3. "Why would Bapa be more effective as a missionary to this people than a person from a foreign field?"

 Lecture
(4 minutes)

Discuss the material in the parallel column concerning idolatry. Have a volunteer read Exodus 20:3 and Deuteronomy 6:5.

Have group members discuss their responses to study guide items 2 and 3.

THE NEED FOR MISSIONS

It seems odd that a world, fashioned by God, must be told about its Creator. But it does. As we learned earlier, all people have sinned and all can be saved. Therein lies the reason for missions and missionaries.

What is a missionary? In the broadest sense of the term, a missionary is a person sent on a mission or errand. In a more restricted sense, a missionary is a person sent forth with the mission of preaching the gospel of Christ so that people who need Christ might be saved.

The need for missionaries is as old as sin, which produced the need for salvation. Whenever and wherever people have sinned, they have needed to be told about Christ.

1. Read Romans 1:20-25. Why do people need God?

_____

_____

What is God's response to their desires?_____

_____

The people of the world knew about God at one time. They knew Him as their Creator and yet they still turned away from Him. They exchanged the glory of God for the images of animals and people. And they taught their children in the same way.

Traditional idol worship is only one way people today choose to turn their backs on their Creator. The world offers a variety of distractions to pull people away from God. Idolatry is defined as anything someone allows to take priority over his or her relationship with the one true God. Our relationship to God is to be first in our lives; anything that takes His place becomes an object of worship or an idol. (See Exodus 20:3 and Deuteronomy 6:5.) For ease of reading, the terms *idol(s)*, *idolatry*, and *idol worship* will be used to refer to those things to which people give more attention than to God.

2. What are some specific things that have become idols within our present culture?

_____

_____

_____

_____

3. Read 1 Corinthians 8:4-7. What is the result of generations of people worshiping idols and gods other than the one true God?

_____

_____

_____

God does not force any person to worship Him. If people choose to worship idols instead of God, He will allow them to do so. He will not force himself on anyone.

4. Read Deuteronomy 5:7-9. What is God's emotion concerning idolatry?

_____

Why might He feel this way? _____

What is the consequence of idolatry?_____

How have you seen this worked out in the lives of friends and acquaintances? _____

_____

_____

Idolatry is self-perpetuating. When people choose to worship idols, they are not only choosing idol worship for themselves, but they are also choosing idol worship for their children and their grandchildren. When adults turn to worshiping idols, soon the knowledge of the truth of God is no longer a part of their family heritage, and their children and grandchildren know only idol worship as a way of life. Innocent children suffer when their parents voluntarily turn from God. They are taught the errors of their parents and the truth of God is hidden from their sight.

In Deuteronomy, God warns parents about the lasting effects of their sins. Children of an alcoholic suffer for that person's sins. The family of a convicted criminal is punished because of his or her iniquity. God does not arbitrarily punish children whose parents sin, but He does warn people that their sins do not die with them. Disobedience and unrighteousness are seeds that bear a frightful harvest.

The principle that our actions produce consequences is true in our own lives. Every decision we make has eternal consequences. We should continually seek to find and do God's will. It is not only our own spiritual welfare which depends upon this, but the eternal destiny of our family and our acquaintances.

✎ **5. Read Joshua 24:2. What does this Scripture passage tell us about the spiritual condition of Abraham's people and country?**

_____

Read Genesis 12:1-3. How did God direct Abraham in response to this idolatry? _____

_____

What did God promise Abraham? For what purpose did He draw Abraham out?

_____

_____

_____

Beginning with His appearance to Abraham, God began to reveal himself in a new way to all of humanity through Abraham and his descendants, the Jews. God called Abraham out of idolatry to make a nation which could retain His truth. He promised to bless all the people of the world through Abraham's descendants. The Jews were to be God's missionaries to the idol-worshiping world.

✎ **6. Read Exodus 19:5,6. What was God's ultimate desire for the nation of Israel?**

_____

_____

To be a missionary meant to be different from the rest of the world. God called Israel out of the world to be His special people. The King James Version of Deuteronomy 14:2 and 26:18 says that the Jews were to be a "peculiar" people. If they were going to carry out their mission in life, they had to be unusual by the world's standards, since the world was lost, alienated from God, and living sinful lives.

✎ **7. Read 1 Samuel 8:5-7,19,20. How did Israel want to be perceived?**

_____

_____

Discussion
(3 minutes)
Ask, "How is the self-perpetuating effect of idolatry evident in our society?"

Response
(4 minutes)
Have group members share their responses to study guide item 5.

Read
(2 minutes)
Have a couple of volunteers read Deuteronomy 14:2 and 26:18 from the NIV and the KJV.

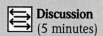

Discussion
(5 minutes)

Have group members share their responses to study guide item 7. Give group members some time to individually consider some ways they might be choosing to be like the world in rejection of what God would really have them do.

Have the group discuss briefly what they think it means to be "peculiar" for God. Have them offer suggestions to be peculiar without being self-righteousness and unapproachable.

Response
(3 minutes)

Have group members share their responses to study guide item 8.

Lecture
(2 minutes)

Discuss the pattern of missionary strategy established in the Bible as presented in the parallel column.

By choosing this behavior, what was Israel doing to God? _____

_____

Israel rejected her opportunity to be a missionary nation. And this choice had grave consequences. Israel could not become like the sinful nations around her without also suffering the penalties reserved by God for sin. Also, the world still needed missionaries to bring the knowledge of God. The nations still needed Him.

If we are to be effective missionaries for Christ, we must be willing to become peculiar in the sense that we glorify God rather than self, material possessions, or physical might. To do this is to become peculiar to our present generation where these things have become worshiped as gods.

THE COMMAND FOR MISSIONS

Who has received the call to become a missionary? Was it merely ancient Israel? Is it only those persons who go from our churches as missionaries to foreign fields? A look at the Bible will show us exactly who Christ has called to be a missionary.

8. Read Matthew 28:19 and Mark 16:15. To whom was Jesus speaking in this passage?

_____

Read Luke 24:45. What did Jesus do for these missionaries before sending them out?

_____

_____

Read Luke 24:49 and Acts 1:8. What did He promise to send to them before they began their ministry?

_____

Read Mark 16:16,17. What signs (of power) would confirm the gospel the disciples preached?

_____

_____

_____

_____

Jesus did not send out these missionaries until they fully understood His message and until they were empowered by the Holy Spirit. He knew the effectiveness of their witness depended on these two things. The Lord also promised to confirm the word they preached with signs and wonders.

9. Read Luke 24:47 and Acts 1:8. What pattern of missionary strategy is given in these passages?

_____

_____

Jesus set forth a definite pattern for missionary growth. After building a strong home church, the disciples could gradually advance their missionary work into the surrounding territory. The eventual goal was to reach the entire world. The Book of Acts shows how the Early Church followed this command quite literally.

10. Read Acts 2:1-4,14. What group of people was being witnessed to in this passage?

_____

_____

Read Acts 8:1. To where was the gospel taken in this verse? _____

_____

Read Acts 11:19,20. Now to where was the gospel taken? _____

_____

The missionary commission was being fulfilled. Jesus' command was being pursued by the 12 apostles and many others.

 11. Read Acts 8:1,4. Who does this passage indicate was preaching the Word?

_____

_____

The missionary command was being fulfilled by every believer who, because of Jewish persecution, had been forced to leave Jerusalem. They shared the Word of God wherever they went. An example of this was Philip, the deacon (Acts 6:5), who carried the gospel to Samaria (Acts 8:5) and many other cities, including Caesarea (Acts 8:40). He also witnessed to the Ethiopian eunuch (Acts 8:26-35).

 12. Read Acts 13:1,2. Who was perhaps the most surprising yet quite effective missionary of the Early Church?

_____

_____

He took the gospel from Antioch throughout Asia Minor and into Europe itself. His call to the Gentiles led him on three separate journeys and took him to much of the Roman Empire.

So the missionary endeavor began with the 12 apostles and extended to all the Christians of the Early Church. It didn't stop there either.

 13. Read Matthew 24:14 and Mark 13:10. When will the missionary effort be completed? Who is responsible to continue this work?

_____

_____

_____

_____

Jesus shared the time when the missionary command would be fulfilled. How will this be accomplished? Can we sit idly by and shrug off our missionary responsibility? Stop and consider what your situation might be if someone hadn't taken the time to share the truth of Jesus with you or your family. Each of us has come to Christ because of a missionary spirit and enthusiasm that always burns where sincere Christians follow the leading of their Lord.

Today, it is our responsibility to obey the command of Christ. Everyone must take the message of Christ's saving grace to the world. We must make God known; we cannot allow ourselves to fail, as Israel did.

 Response
(2 minutes)
Have group members share their responses to study guide item 11.

 Discussion
(5 minutes)
Have group members share their responses to study guide item 13. Then, have them go back to study guide item 8. Ask, "Are these promises for us today? Why or why not?"

Have volunteers read Matthew 10:19,20; John 14:12-16; 17:20-23. These passages should clarify how Jesus intended to spread His message of salvation to all the world.

THE PARTNERSHIP IN MISSIONS

We cannot all leave our homes and go with the gospel, but we can all have a part in the great missionary partnership that encompasses the globe. The missions effort must by supported, financially and with prayer, so some of us must fulfill that task.

In the last session, we looked at the good stewardship of the Macedonian churches. Their generosity earned words of praise from the apostle Paul when he wrote to the Corinthian believers. Probably the most generous of these Macedonian churches was the church at Philippi.

 14. Read Philippians 1:3,5 and 4:10,14-16,18. How does Paul commend the Philippian church?

_____

_____

What indication does he give about their previous involvement in his ministry? _____

_____

How does he describe their missionary giving? _____

_____

The Philippian church adopted the missionary vision of the apostle Paul. They supported him with so much that he reported to them he had more than enough to meet his needs. Their partnership through support allowed him to continue in his ministry.

Through Paul's writing we learn a valuable truth: Those who contribute to missionary programs are partners with the missionaries in obeying the command of Christ recorded in Matthew 28:19. We can't all physically go to the field—home or abroad—but we can go through the vehicle of missionary giving.

 15. Read Philippians 4:17-19. According to Paul, what benefits will come to those who support missions?

_____

_____

Paul knew that the Christians who liberally give to support God's work will share in the eternal rewards. Missionary offerings are gifts that produce fruit that may never be realized until we all get to heaven.

It is part of our Christian responsibility to give and pray for missions and missionaries. Every missionary on the field needs many people at home praying and giving. By doing this, we become partners with those missionaries. The Lord may not call each of us to relocate to a mission field, but we are not excused from all missionary responsibility just because of the lack of a specific calling.

SUMMARY

Jesus has given a command to preach His gospel in all the world. The apostles and the Early Church started the missionary effort. Believers throughout history have perpetuated it. We must take up the responsibility to continue the effort to reach our world.

We must remember that we live our lives only once, as do the many lost people around us and far away from us. We have only one chance to serve Christ in this life. Some will have a call from the Lord to go to the mission field. But those who do not receive the call to go should take advantage of opportunities to pray for and give to missionaries and the missionary efforts in which they are involved. By doing so, they will later reap an eternal and abundant harvest.

 Response
(3 minutes)
Have group members share their responses to study guide item 14.

 Handout
(3 minutes)
Distribute a copy of resource 11B, "The Partnership Of Missions," to each group member. Have them read the story and discuss the importance of those who give to those who go.

 Response
(2 minutes)
Have group members share their responses to study guide item 15.

 Summary
(3 minutes)
Distribute the list of the missionaries your church supports, home and foreign. Challenge group members to begin to support these missionaries with prayer or finances. If your church has newsletters from the missionaries, share some of them with group members.

LET'S REVIEW

 1. What is idolatry?

_____

_____

_____

_____

 2. How did idolatry come into existence?

_____

_____

_____

3. Why did God establish the nation of Israel through Abraham?

_____

_____

_____

_____

4. How were the Israelites to behave? (See Deuteronomy 14:2 and 26:18, KJV.) How should we behave in our society?

_____

_____

_____

_____

5. To whom does the missionary command in Matthew 28:19 and Mark 16:15 apply?

_____

_____

_____

6. How can we all be involved in the missionary command?

_____

_____

_____

_____

Review
(3 minutes)

Select two or three study guide items from the "Let's Review" section to check the comprehension level of group members. If understanding of the study material seems weak, recommend that individuals work through the study again.

Closing Prayer
(2 minutes)

Pray that God would show each individual a way to respond to the command to be actively involved in missions and that the Holy Spirit would provide the power to follow through with that response.

Discussion
(3 minutes)

Ask the group for concrete suggestions concerning future topics of study. Consider, perhaps, additional titles in the _Spiritual Discovery Series_. These are available from your _Radiant Life_ distributor.

Try to make a decision at this session so that study materials can be ordered and possibly brought to one of the next two sessions.

Preparing For Next Session

Remind group members to complete study 12 before the next session.

Talk with your pastor, before the next session, about the possibility of in-depth personal evangelism training through your church.

Group Fellowship
(5 minutes)

Invite individuals to share in fellowship and refreshments before they leave.

STUDY 12

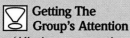

Study Objective

To review keys of personal evangelism and become active in witnessing for Christ.

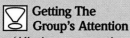

What You Will Need

☐ Enough copies of resources 12A, "Step-By-Step," and 12B, "Know The Scripture," for each individual.

☐ An overhead projector, blank transparencies, and markers.

☐ A sign-up sheet for group members interested in more in-depth personal evangelism training. This is just for gathering names of interested individuals. Talk with your pastor before the session about the possibility of such training through your church.

Getting The Group's Attention

(All times are estimates. 8 minutes)

Distribute a copy of resource 12A, "Step-By-Step," to each group member. Give them 3 minutes to read the handout.

Ask, "How is making friendship bread similar to sharing the gospel?" (What happens to the batter if you don't follow the instructions exactly, step-by-step?)

State: "As we learn to listen to the leading of the Lord, He will guide us to opportunities and provide us with the words to say. But we have to be willing to receive instructions a step at a time and follow them without hesitation."

WITNESSING FOR CHRIST

When people surrender their lives to Christ, they take possession of the greatest gift available—the gospel of Jesus Christ. This is not a gift to be hoarded. Jesus has commanded believers to share His gospel with the whole world.

Every Christian is sent out by Christ to proclaim the good news. We are evangelists—bearers of glad tidings.

Witnessing is a bit of a scary endeavor to most of us though. But it becomes less intimidating as we learn more about God and the Scriptures and become sensitive to the voice of the Holy Spirit to direct us to opportunities. We need to understand being a witness is a privilege. We are representatives of the Almighty Lord, sharing His life-saving gift. We must be obedient to Christ's command. God will change people's lives.

Transition Statement ➡ The biblical account of Philip the evangelist provides three keys for successful personal evangelism.

OBEY THE LORD

Obedience to the Lord is one key to successful witnessing for Christ. If we are to become successful witnesses for Christ, we must not only obey Christ by witnessing, but we must also obey Him in other ways. An example of someone who obeyed God is Philip.

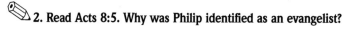 **1. Read Acts 21:8. What title is given to Philip?**

_____

Read Acts 6:3-5. How else might Philip have been identified?

_____

_____

_____

Philip's title is a recognition of the kind of man he was. Above all else, he was an evangelist. Although he was a man of many good characteristics (Acts 6:3), he was known best by none of these other characteristics. Whatever else he was, Philip was an evangelist.

What is an evangelist? Today we think of an evangelist as a person who travels from church to church holding special services, but this is not the complete meaning of the word *evangelist*. Our word *evangelist* is a word which is transliterated or borrowed from the Greek language. The Greek word which we have borrowed is *euangelistes* which means "one who announces glad tidings" or "one who proclaims good news" or "one who preaches the gospel." Any Christian who tells others of the gospel of the Lord Jesus Christ is an evangelist, whether that person is a man or a woman, a boy or a girl.

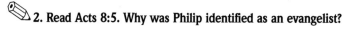 **2. Read Acts 8:5. Why was Philip identified as an evangelist?**

_____

_____

Philip was "sent" to Samaria due to the persecution of the church in Jerusalem. Regardless of Philip's motivation, he obeyed Christ by preaching of Him wherever he was. The good news of Christ is still the only truly good news we can proclaim to the world around us. People today are groping fearfully through dark times, uncertain about so many things, and other individuals are trying to give words of hope to the world. But the hope they offer is temporary and weak. The only true message of hope is the gospel of Jesus Christ.

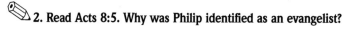 **3. Think about a person who is in deep trouble and needs the hope offered through Jesus. Write that person's name below. Pray for an opportunity to share the gospel message with him or her.**

_____

Philip became an evangelist as did every other member of the Church during that time. It's no wonder the Church grew so rapidly in its early days! Imagine what might happen if each of us did our part in evangelizing our world. Philip was an evangelist among evangelists. Even though every member of the Church is an evangelist, Philip is referred to as "Philip, the evangelist."

 4. Read Acts 8:6-8,12. What resulted from Philip's ministry in Samaria?

_____

_____

_____

 Overhead
(2 minutes)
Place a blank transparency on the projector and write at the top, "Keys To Successful Witnessing." Then, write the numeral 1 and "Obedience To The Lord" below the heading.

 Discussion
(5 minutes)
Have group members share their responses to study guide item 1.
Discuss the definition of *evangelist* as presented in the material in the parallel column.
Ask, "Using this definition, who is an evangelist?"

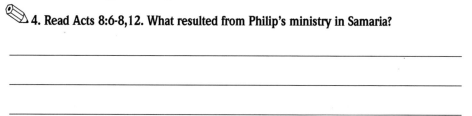 **Brainstorm**
(6 minutes)
Have group members share their responses to study guide item 4.
Discuss briefly the paragraph immediately following study guide item 4.
Have group members brainstorm situations unbelievers are dealing with that could be helped by sharing Jesus with those people. As they share their responses, write them on a blank transparency.

The Samaritan people had many problems—many were sick, many were demon-possessed, and they were unhappy. Philip did not merely deal with the symptoms. He went to the core of their problems—sin. He preached the good news that Jesus Christ can save, heal, and deliver. By doing this, Philip brought the message that could transform lives.

How many times have we honestly given the message our neighbor or acquaintance has needed? Have we truly told that person about Jesus Christ? If not, we have not been evangelists. We may have been sympathetic, comforting, helpful, and kind. And these are qualities every Christian should exhibit. But above all else, we must be witnesses. We must tell others that Jesus Christ came to remove sin from people's lives, and to prepare them for heaven.

 5. Read Acts 8:14-17. What happened next to the church in Samaria?

_____

_____

How might what was happening in Samaria be described today? _____

The news of Philip's success as a witness for Christ carried to Jerusalem. It was important for the believers in Samaria to be fully equipped to be witnesses themselves. The apostles did not want them to be without the power of the Holy Spirit.

The success in Samaria occurred because Philip obeyed the Lord. Jesus had commanded Christians to go into all the world and proclaim the gospel. Philip had obeyed the Lord, proclaiming the good news in Samaria.

After such a successful campaign, we might expect Philip to relax and feel he had done his part. But his obedience to the Lord did not end in Samaria.

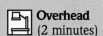 6. Read Acts 8:26,27. What direction did Philip receive?

_____

_____

How did Philip respond? _____

The Lord presented Philip with another opportunity to obey Him. And again he obeyed. The Scripture text in Acts 8:27 implies an immediate response to do what God had directed him. Both verbs used in the text are in the Greek aorist tense, which suggests prompt obedience. So in the midst of a revival in Samaria, Philip removed himself and went down to the southernmost desert road which joined Jerusalem with Gaza.

If we are to be successful witnesses for Christ, we must learn to obey God's leading. We cannot say that tomorrow will be as good a time as today to speak to that friend about Christ. If the Spirit impresses us to speak now, we must immediately obey. We cannot tell what is going on in the heart of that person. Only God knows. If He tells us to act, we had better obey. As we obey God's directions, He will provide opportunities for us to witness just as He provided opportunities for Philip. Continued successful soul winning demands obedience to the Lord. Philip obeyed the Lord.

The Ethiopian eunuch was to provide Philip with another opportunity to witness for Christ, although that was not yet known to Philip. Philip was to receive that opportunity because he obeyed the Lord.

LISTEN TO THE SPIRIT

Another key to successful soul winning is listening to the directions of the Holy Spirit. When the Holy Spirit speaks, we must listen.

Notice that when the Lord guided Philip, He did not tell him everything at once. The angel which appeared to Philip merely told him to go. Philip had to obey God's first instructions before he received any further direction.

Philip obeyed the Lord and proceeded to the desert road which connected Jerusalem with Gaza. When he arrived at that road, Philip did not know what the Lord would have

Response
(2 minutes)

Have group members share their responses to study guide item 5.

Discussion
(4 minutes)

Have an individual share his or her response to study guide item 6.

Discuss the implication of the first half of Acts 8:27, referring to the timing of Philip's obedience. Use the material in the parallel column to enhance this discussion.

Overhead
(2 minutes)

Place the overhead you entitled "Keys To Successful Witnessing" back on the projector. Now write the numeral 2 and "Listening To The Holy Spirit" below the previous item.

Discuss the material provided in the parallel column regarding obeying God one step at a time.

him to do next. He saw a chariot traveling in the direction of Egypt, and in the chariot, a man reading out loud. Still Philip did not know what the Lord wanted him to do.

✎ 7. Read Acts 8:29,30. What instruction did Philip receive from the Holy Spirit?

_____

_____

What was Philip's reaction to the Holy Spirit's direction? _____

Philip was sensitive to the voice, or the leading, of the Holy Spirit. He did not hesitate to obey the Spirit's direction. Philip still did not know exactly what he was supposed to do, but he was willing to let the Lord lead him one step at a time. The Lord had commanded him to come to this road; he had obeyed. The Holy Spirit commanded him to glue himself to the chariot; he would obey. Philip knew that the Holy Spirit was leading him and would continue to lead him.

Some Christians never witness because they are afraid they will not know the right thing to say. They want to know at the very beginning how the whole thing is going to turn out. God does not always tell us this. He gives us one step to take at a time. We have to walk in faith, following the Spirit. But when we do this, we will be amazed at how marvelously everything works out.

Sensitivity to the voice of the Holy Spirit is a quality which should be cultivated by every witness for Christ. We cannot obey Christ unless we hear Him speak through His Spirit. When He speaks, we must obey Him unquestioningly. He is able to lead us to the right place at the right time to meet the right person. If we hesitate or delay, we might lose an opportunity; we might lose a soul along with it. When the Holy Spirit says, "Go," we must do just that. Our obedience to the promptings of the Holy Spirit will help to make us effective witnesses.

USE THE SCRIPTURES

The man riding in the chariot was an Ethiopian. He was an important man in his country, being in charge of the treasury of the queen of Ethiopia. He was returning to Ethiopia after having been to Jerusalem.

✎ 8. Read Acts 8:27,28. Why had the Ethiopian been to Jerusalem?

_____

What was the Ethiopian doing when Philip was told to go to him? _____

_____

What can we infer about the condition of the Ethiopian's heart from this passage?

_____

_____

_____

Because of Philip's obedience to the Lord and the Spirit's leading, he was now at the right place at the right time to witness to the Ethiopian. God knew exactly when the Ethiopian would be reading the Book of Isaiah, and He knew he would have difficulty understanding the passage. God sent Philip to help the Ethiopian understand.

✎ 9. Read Acts 8:30,31,34. What did Philip ask the Ethiopian when he heard him reading out loud?

_____

Response
(2 minutes)
Have group members share their responses to study guide item 7.

Testimonies
(5 minutes)
Have volunteers share experiences they have had when they had to trust God for step-by-step guidance in witnessing or in any other circumstance.

Discussion
(3 minutes)
Ask, "How do we know when the Spirit speaks to us? Does He always speak in the same way?"

Response
(3 minutes)
Have group members share their responses to study guide item 8.
If not revealed by individuals' responses to the third part of the study guide item, share that the inference should be that the Ethiopian was searching for the truth. He had probably already converted to Judaism and was now seeking even more.

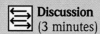
Discussion
(3 minutes)

Discuss the significance of the verbal exchange between Philip and the eunuch as presented in study guide item 9.

State: "Philip didn't just stand by the chariot. He asked if help was needed and then listened to the Ethiopian's questions. Why is that important?"

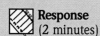
Response
(2 minutes)

Have group members share their responses to study guide item 10.

Overhead
(2 minutes)

Write on your "Keys To Successful Witnessing" overhead the numeral 3 and "Knowing And Using The Scripture."

Handout
(2 minutes)

Distribute a copy of resource 12B, "Know The Scripture," to each group member. Challenge everyone to memorize and study for understanding the passages on the handout.

Summary
(3 minutes)

Have group members make a self-evaluation of their readiness to witness: Are they scripturally solid? Are they willing to obey? Are they able to hear the Spirit speak to them?

Let group members know about the sign-up sheet for more training in personal evangelism. Give them the information you received from your pastor regarding the possibility of such training through your church.

What was the Ethiopian's response? What question did he ask Philip? _____

_____

An unsaved person may not always recognize the plan of salvation from reading the Bible. Sometimes a Christian is needed to explain the need for salvation and exactly how to be saved. We need to consider our own conversions. Did we come to Christ by simply reading the Bible, or did another Christian guide us? Christ did not leave just the Word in the world to spread the gospel; He left Spirit-filled Christians who love the Word to preach, teach, and witness. Philip was such a person.

Philip, the evangelist, did not have to be asked twice. The Lord had commanded him; the Spirit had spoken to him; the Ethiopian had asked him. So Philip shared Christ.

10. Read Acts 8:35-38. How did Philip share the truth of Christ with the Ethiopian?

_____

What was the result of Philip's witnessing? _____

Philip was able to use the Scripture in witnessing because he knew the Scripture. He was able to help the Ethiopian understand the Scripture because he himself understood the Scripture. If Philip had not known Isaiah was prophesying of Christ, he could not have answered the eunuch's sincere inquiry.

Knowing and using the Scripture is an additional key to evangelism. This is the most effective way we can witness. Sure we can tell others about our personal experiences, but we must also be able to point hungry souls to the Word of God. How familiar are we with the Bible? Would we be able to sit down with someone and share God's plan for redemption using the Scripture as our guide?

Philip was able to make an excellent presentation of the gospel using the Isaiah passage the eunuch was reading even though it had been written about 700 years before Christ. The passage from Isaiah 52:13 to 53:12 is sometimes called the "gospel in prophecy."

11. Read Isaiah 53:4-6,10. Identify which verse(s) in this passage relate to the key elements of the gospel message listed below.

All have sinned.— _____

All deserve punishment.— _____

Christ took our punishment.— _____

We can make Christ our offering for sin and obtain life.— _____

This passage tells us we should pay the penalty for our own sins, but instead, Christ has died in order that we might go free. This is the good news! No one needs to go into hell because of his or her own sins. To be saved, each person must individually accept Christ's death as payment for his or her sins. Then, live so as to please the Savior.

SUMMARY

Witnessing for Christ is an act of obedience to Christ's command to preach the gospel to all people. As we become obedient to God's leading and sensitive to the direction of the Holy Spirit, we will find there are a lot of opportunities to witness—a lot of hurting, searching people.

How can we improve our obedience and ability to follow the Holy Spirit's leading? We must develop our relationship with God by spending time talking with Him, reading His Word (Him talking to us), and giving Him the opportunity to guide us by learning to be still and listen. Then we will be able to see the opportunities to help people understand the good news and lead those individuals to Christ.

LET'S REVIEW

1. Define *evangelist.* Specifically, who is an evangelist?

_____

_____

_____

_____

2. What are the three keys to successful witnessing outlined in this study?

_____

_____

_____

3. What did Philip preach in Samaria? What were the results?

_____

_____

_____

_____

4. What can we learn about God's direction and timing and the witness' obedience from the account of the Ethiopian eunuch in Acts 8:26-37?

_____

_____

_____

_____

_____

5. How can Christians develop the three key traits of a successful witness?

_____

_____

_____

_____

_____

_____

Review
(3 minutes)

Select two or three study guide items from the "Let's Review" section to review the material in this study. If comprehension seems lacking, suggest individuals reread the study.

Closing Prayer
(2 minutes)

Lead the group in a prayer of commitment to personal evangelism.

Discussion
(2 minutes)

If a decision regarding the next topic of study for the group has not yet been made, try to come to a consensus so that study material can be ordered. Other titles from the *Spiritual Discovery Series* can be ordered from your *Radiant Life* distributor.

Preparing For Next Session

Remind group members to complete study 13 before the next session.

Arrange for a group member to make a brief report on the events that will follow the Rapture, using a pre-tribulation view, up to the revelation of Christ. (See resource 13C for help identifying these events.)

Arrange for a group member to make a brief report on the events that will follow the revelation of Christ, using a pre-millennial view, up to the new heavens and earth. (See resource 13C for help identifying these events.)

Group Fellowship
(5 minutes)

Encourage everyone to have refreshments and fellowship together before leaving.

STUDY 13

Study Objective

To contemplate the imminence of Christ's second coming and live in such a way to be ready and win others to Christ.

What You Will Need

☐ Paper and a writing instrument for each individual.
☐ Enough copies of resources 13A, "Various Views Of The Rapture," and 13B, "Views Of The Millennium," for each group member.
☐ A group member to make a brief report on the events that will follow the Rapture, using a pre-tribulation view, up to the revelation of Christ (see resource 13C for help identifying these events).
☐ A group member to briefly report on the events that will follow the revelation of Christ, from the premillennial view, up to the new heavens and earth (see resource 13C for help identifying these events).
☐ An overhead projector.
☐ An overhead transparency of resource 13C, "Panorama Of Prophecy."

Getting The Group's Attention

(All times are estimates. 5 minutes)

Distribute a piece of paper and a writing instrument to each group member.

Ask, "If Christ returned today, whom do you know that would not be ready to meet Him?"

Have individuals write the names on the papers given to them. Have them write today's date next to each name and label another column, "Date Saved." The idea is to pray daily for each individual on the list and record the date each one comes to know the Lord.

Encourage group members to add names of people as they think of them.

THE SECOND COMING OF CHRIST

Christians have looked forward to the second coming of Christ ever since He ascended into heaven to sit at the right hand of the Father. Christ's second coming is the precious hope of the Church. Songs and sermons have been written about Christ's second coming throughout Christian history.

Jesus did not set a time for His return to earth. Through the ages, Christians have hoped He might come during their lifetime. They have endeavored to obey Christ's instructions to "watch and pray" in anticipation of the day when He will break through the heavens in His triumphant return.

He has not yet returned, but the day of His coming is nearer now than when He first promised to come back. Signs of the times indicate the nearness of His return more vividly than ever before. We may be the ones who are alive when Christ returns!

Transition Statement ➡ Recognizing the urgency of Christ's return will help Christians live righteously.

THE FACT OF HIS COMING

Jesus mentioned the fact of the Second Coming many times prior to His death and resurrection. The number of times He mentioned the Second Coming gives some indication of its importance in the plan of God.

Jesus began referring to the Second Coming at Caesarea Philippi, about 6 months before His death.

✎ **1. Read Matthew 16:27. What does this passage teach us about the Second Coming?**

_____

_____

Jesus began teaching about the Second Coming when He began teaching about His death. While His death meant He would be absent from His disciples, the Second Coming meant that Christ would return for His disciples. One would introduce a period of separation; the other will conclude the period of separation.

✎ **2. Read John 14:3. How does Jesus join the teachings concerning His leaving and returning in this Scripture passage?**

_____

_____

After Caesarea Philippi, Jesus referred to the Second Coming many times. Some of those times were in direct statements; others of them were in parables.

✎ **3. Read Matthew 24:3-28; Luke 12:35-40; 17:22-35; and 19:12-27. What instructions does Jesus give His disciples regarding His second coming?**

_____

_____

_____

_____

_____

The fact of Christ's second coming was confirmed often after His death, resurrection, and ascension. The apostles often referred to it with confirmation and exhortation.

✎ **4. Read Hebrews 10:37; James 5:7,8; 1 Peter 1:4-13; 4:13; 5:4; 2 Peter 3:3-18; 1 John 3:2; Jude 14,15; Revelation 1:7; 3:11; 22:7,12,20. In what specific ways did the apostles encourage or instruct the Church regarding Jesus' second coming?**

_____

_____

_____

_____

_____

_____

_____

Lecture
(2 minutes)
Lead the group in a discussion of the material in the parallel column beginning with "The Facts Of His Coming" through study guide item 2.

Discussion
(7 minutes)
Have group members share their responses to study guide item 3.

Have individuals turn to Matthew 24:3-28 and consider the indicators of end-times that Jesus shared with His disciples.

Ask the following questions:

1. "How many of these indicators are evident in today's society?" (Give ample time to discuss each indicator.)

2. "What is being done about Jesus' statement in verse 14?"

3. "What do our responses to the two preceding questions tell us about the timing of the return of Jesus?"

The writers of these books of the Bible encouraged the believers of the Early Church, but they also provide encouragement and direction for us. The New Testament is full of affirmations of Jesus' return which we can hold on to with hope.

5. Read 1 Corinthians 1:8; 15:22-28,35,49-58; Philippians 3:20; 1 Timothy 6:13-16; 2 Timothy 4:8; Titus 2:11-13. What further witness of the Second Coming does Paul give in these Scripture passages?

_____

_____

_____

_____

Response
(2 minutes)
Have group members share their responses to study guide item 5.

This vast array of Scripture passages speaking of the return of the Lord Jesus Christ is convincing proof that the Second Coming was an accepted fact by the New Testament writers. Not only did they accept it as a fact, but they wanted others to accept it as a fact. Regardless of how long Christ tarries, He will come. Just as Christ came the first time as the Messiah, He will come again.

THE NATURE OF HIS COMING

How will the Lord return? In what manner will He come back to earth? These questions have occupied many people. The Bible speaks clearly concerning the nature of Christ's return. We don't have to guess about it. At the time of Jesus' ascension, the two men who spoke to the disciples told them two important facts about how He would return.

6. Read Acts 1:9-11. What does the phrase "this same Jesus" mean? (See 1 Thessalonians 4:16 for help.)

_____

_____

Lecture
(2 minutes)
Discuss the nature of Jesus' return using the material in the parallel column, including study guide item 6.

The understanding of this phrase is extremely important. Uncertainty has caused a variety of misconceptions regarding the Second Coming. The Bible clearly refutes each argument for an alternative view of Jesus' literal, physical second coming.

Some contend the Second Coming occurs for each Christian as he or she dies.

7. Read 1 Thessalonians 4:13-18. Who (living, dead, or both) will be a part of the Second Coming?

_____

_____

How does knowing who will be a part of the Second Coming negate the argument that each Christian experiences the Second Coming upon dying?

_____

_____

_____

On whose authority does Paul give this information (v. 15)? _____

_____

Response
(3 minutes)
Have group members share their responses to study guide item 7.

Others believe the Second Coming refers to the coming of the Holy Spirit.

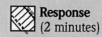

8. Read John 14:16,26; 16:7; and Acts 2:32,33. How do these passages demonstrate the Second Coming is separate from the coming of the Holy Spirit?

_____

_____

_____

The absence of Jesus was vital to the coming of the Holy Spirit. Because the Bible clearly teaches it will be Jesus who returns, the Second Coming cannot involve the coming of the Holy Spirit. The Holy Spirit was sent while Jesus was at the right hand of the Father in heaven.

Because of how they interpret prophecy, some hold that the destruction of Jerusalem in A.D. 70 by the Roman armies was the Second Coming. When this destruction occurred, the people fled the city. The act of fleeing implies fear.

9. Read 2 Timothy 4:8; Titus 2:13; Hebrews 9:28; 1 Peter 5:4; 2 Peter 3:13; 1 John 3:2,3. What picture of the Second Coming do these Scripture passages paint?

_____

_____

_____

We know it will be Jesus who returns in the Second Coming. But in what form will He appear?

10. Reread Acts 1:9-11. The phrase "in like manner" (KJV) or "in the same way" (NIV) refers to the form Jesus will have when He reappears. In what form will Jesus return (spiritual or physical)? (See Luke 13:35 and 21:27 for help.)

_____

_____

_____

His return will also be visible. The angelic being at the Ascension proclaimed Jesus would return in the same way He left.

11. Read Luke 13:35; 21:27. How does Jesus describe His return?

_____

_____

_____

Just as the disciples saw Him ascend into heaven, those who are on earth when He returns will see Him appear in the sky. Christ, at His second coming, will return personally, bodily, and visibly.

THE PHASES OF HIS COMING

There are two phases of Christ's second coming. The first phase is His return for the Church. This return for the Church is often called the Rapture. The word *rapture* means "carry away." Thus the reference to the Church's carrying away is called the Rapture.

As was discovered earlier in this study, both the righteous dead and the living members of the Church will be a part of the Second Coming. They will be participants in the Rapture phase. Jesus will return for all who have ever been a part of His Church, whether still alive or those who have already died.

 Response (2 minutes)
Have a few individuals share their responses to study guide item 8.

 Discussion (3 minutes)
Have group members share their responses to study guide item 9.
Ask, "How does the picture of the Second Coming painted in these passages prove the Second Coming did not occur when Jerusalem was destroyed in A.D. 70?"

Response (3 minutes)
Have individuals share their responses to study guide items 10 and 11.

 Handout (3 minutes)
Distribute a copy of resource 13A, "Various Views Of The Rapture," to each group member. Briefly discuss the three views presented.

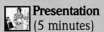
Presentation
(5 minutes)
Introduce the group member who prepared the report on post-Rapture events up to the revelation of Christ. Allow some time following the report for group discussion.

Response
(4 minutes)
Have group members share their responses to study guide items 12 and 13.

Handout
(3 minutes)
Distribute a copy of resource 13B, "Views Of The Millennium," to each group member. Briefly discuss the three views presented.

Presentation
(5 minutes)
Introduce the group member who prepared the report on post-Revelation events up to the new heavens and earth. Allow some time following the report for group discussion.

Response
(2 minutes)
Have group members share their responses to study guide item 14.

✎ **12. Read 1 Thessalonians 4:15-17. What will happen to the bodies of the dead in Christ at the Second Coming?**

_____

_____

What about those believers who are alive at the time of the Second Coming? _____

_____

When Paul originally wrote to the Thessalonians, he was responding to their fears that those who died before Christ returned would have no hope for eternity. He wanted them to know there would be a bodily resurrection for those believers who had died.

Paul wrote to the Corinthians, also, concerning the resurrection of the righteous dead.

✎ **13. Read 1 Corinthians 15:42-44,49. What do these passages say about the bodies of the righteous dead when they are resurrected?**

_____

_____

_____

Read 1 Corinthians 15:51-53. When Christ returns, what will happen to those believers who are still alive?

_____

_____

Read 1 John 3:2. What will our imperishable bodies be like? _____

_____

If we are Christ's, whether we be dead or alive at His coming, we will be raptured to be with Him. We will be made like Him, in the spiritual sense. We are a part of His Church and will always be with Him.

During this first phase of Christ's return, the Church is caught up to meet Him in the clouds. At that time Christ does not actually come down to the earth.

The second phase of the Second Coming occurs sometime later. This is frequently called the Revelation. At that time, Christ returns to the earth as King. (See Zechariah 14:9.) At that time, Christ will establish the Jewish nation as a kingdom, and rule for a millennium or a thousand years. Christians who believe that Jesus will come for the Church before the millennial kingdom is established are known as "premillennialists."

THE TIMING OF HIS COMING

It seems the normal question to ask when we study the second coming of Christ is, "When is this going to take place?" People throughout history, since Jesus' ascension, have tried to answer this question. They have published formulas and set dates naming the day and the hour of Christ's return.

✎ **14. Read Mark 13:32 and Acts 1:6,7. What does Jesus say about the timing of His return?**

_____

_____

The important thing is not that we know *when* He will return; the important thing is that we know He *will* return.

 15. Read Mark 13:33 and 2 Peter 3:10-14. Because we are certain of the Lord's return, how are we to behave?

_____

_____

_____

How might knowing the exact date and time of Christ's return affect our behavior?

_____

_____

_____

Knowing that Christ will return, we have no reason to allow His second coming to catch us by surprise. We should live so that we will be ready when He comes. God wants His followers to be ready at all times.

 16. Read 1 Thessalonians 5:9. What do we know about the timing of the Rapture, and therefore the Second Coming? What will it precede?

_____

_____

God does not wish that any should have to endure His wrath. He loves every individual who has ever lived. Some think since Jesus has not yet returned He never will.

 17. Read 2 Peter 3:9. What explanation does this verse give us for God's delaying Christ's return?

_____

_____

What should our reaction be to this knowledge? _____

_____

_____

SUMMARY

As we look ahead to the second coming of Christ, our hearts leap with joy. Christ's return will mean the end of sorrows and trials for all believers. Although we don't know the time of His return, we live in confidence that He will return. We should live in such a way we will not be caught unaware. We should be watching for His physical, visible return.

But what will become of the unsaved? For them, Christ's return brings tragedy because it is the beginning of final judgment. God will delay as long as possible to allow people the opportunity to know Him. We have a responsibility to take the good news of God's salvation to all those who need to hear. Christ's return is inevitable. It is up to each individual Christian how the time leading up to His return will be spent. Let's work to lead others to Christ and watch for His return!

Response
(2 minutes)
Have group members share their responses to study guide item 15.

Overhead
(3 minutes)
Display the transparency of resource 13C, "Panorama Of Prophecy." Briefly review the events depicted on the resource using the information shared in the two reports given earlier in the session. Explain that this resource is based on a pre-Tribulation, premillennial point of view of the Rapture.

Discussion
(3 minutes)
Have group members share their responses to study guide item 17. Have individuals refer back to the lists of names they compiled at the beginning of the session. Remind them to pray daily for each person on their lists.

Summary
(2 minutes)
State: "We have examined the biblical basis for a lot of principles over many weeks during this study. Hold on to your books and use them as references in the future. You might use your book to help someone else understand the biblical basis of a principle. Remember, if you are looking for an answer to a problem or question, the Bible is your best source."

LET'S REVIEW

1. How do we know Jesus is coming again?

_____

_____

_____

2. Why did Jesus associate His second coming with His teaching concerning His death?

_____

_____

_____

3. Explain the nature of Christ's return.

_____

_____

_____

_____

4. What will happen to the bodies of the righteous dead and to those who are alive in Christ during the first phase of His coming?

_____

_____

_____

_____

5. When will Christ return? How should we live in light of this timing?

_____

_____

_____

_____

 Review
(3 minutes)

Select two or three study guide items from the "Let's Review" section to review the material in this study. If comprehension seems lacking, suggest individuals reread the study.

 Closing Prayer
(2 minutes)

Pray that the Holy Spirit would guide our living so that we will be ready when Jesus returns for the Church. Ask God to help us be bold witnesses for Him until that time comes.

Preparing For Next Session

Finalize the selection for the group's next topical study. If study materials are already available, distribute them to the group and encourage them to begin working on study 1.

If the group has decided to quit meeting together, plan a get-together for the upcoming week.

Group Fellowship
(5 minutes)

Encourage everyone to have refreshments and fellowship together before leaving.

What Do You Believe?

Respond to the following questions as completely as you can. There is no need to put your name on this work sheet. It is going to be used to generate discussion and give the leader an overview of the ideas and beliefs of the group as a whole which will help in the remaining sessions.

1. How would you describe your current spiritual relationship with God?

_____

_____

_____

2. What, in your opinion, is most important to maintaining a right relationship with God?

_____

_____

_____

3. Have you been baptized in water? By what method were you baptized?

_____

_____

4. Have you received the baptism in the Holy Spirit? If yes, describe your experience, initial and continuing. If no, are you interested in being baptized in the Spirit?

_____

_____

_____

5. What do you believe about divine healing?

_____

_____

_____

6. What is your definition of stewardship?

_____

_____

_____

7. What do you see as your responsibility in reaching the world for Christ?

_____

_____

_____

8. Briefly write out your understanding of the second coming of Jesus.

_____

_____

_____

_____

AGREE/DISAGREE

1. God does not send people to hell.

2. God never intended for people to go to hell (Matthew 25:41).

3. God's justice demands punishment for sin.

4. God takes no personal pleasure in sentencing anyone to eternal torment (Ezekiel 33:11).

5. God wants to provide everyone with an opportunity to know Him (2 Peter 3:9).

The Lost Sons

Luke 15:11-32

The Younger Son (vv. 12-24)	The Elder Son (vv. 25-32)
1. Took his share (v. 12)	1. Made his way to the house (vv. 25-27)
2. Took his leave (v. 13)	A. Heard music and dancing
A. Left his home	B. Heard brother was home
B. Left his God	C. Heard his father had honored his brother
3. Found a job (vv. 14-16)	2. Made father come to him (v. 28)
4. Found himself (vv. 17-19)	3. Argued with his father (vv. 29,30)
A. Realized his father's servants were better off	A. I was faithful
B. Realized his sin was against his father and his God	B. I wasn't honored
C. Realized he needed to humble himself	C. My brother was unfaithful and disobedient
5. Lost son returned to father (vv. 20,21)	D. Why do you honor him?
A. Father ran to greet him	4. Father's answer (vv. 31,32)
B. Son hurried to humble himself	A. You never left me.
6. Father returned all son had lost (vv. 22-24)	B. You enjoy all I have.
A. Symbols of a son	C. Your brother returned as if from the dead.
B. Food of a son	D. Your brother will receive no more than you.
C. Life of a son	

Population Census

World Population (1995 estimate)—5,757,300,000

Christian population (Professing Christians)—30.1% of world population

There are 237 countries in the world with 11,874 distinct, ethnolinguistic people groups.
   Of the 237 countries, 149 have a professing Christian population of more than 50%.
   Of the people groups, 3,915 are considered unevangelized or unreached.

There are 6,528 different languages spoken.
   The whole Bible has been published in only 276 of these languages. But this does make up 76% of the world's population.
   The New Testament is available in 676 additional languages.
   Portions of the Scriptures are available in 1,012 other languages.
   That leaves 4,564 groups with no Scripture in their own language. This means that the people who speak two-thirds of the languages of the world make up only 6% of its population.
   There are translations in progress for 1,199 languages.

Definitions:
   Professing Christians—All people who claim an allegiance to a Christian denomination. This number includes those individuals who claim Christianity based on the definition of their country as a Christian nation. Therefore, not all in this number are truly born-again Christians.
   Ethnolinguistic—A person's identity and primary loyalty is defined according to language and/or ethnicity.
   Unreached people group—An ethnolinguistic people among whom there is no viable indigenous community of believing Christians with adequate numbers and resources to evangelize their own people without outside (cross-cultural) help. Also referred to as "hidden people" or "frontier people group." This term is based on a measurement of *exposure* of a people group to the gospel and not on a measurement of the *response* to the gospel shared.

Source: Patrick Johnstone, *Operation World*, Zondervan Publishing House, 1993.

Why Water Baptism?

The Scripture references listed below give us some insight into the relevance and method of water baptism. Look up each reference in the left-hand column and match it up with the proper identifying phrase in the right-hand column. As you go through these Scripture passages, come to a personal conclusion as to the reason for and method of water baptism.

Matthew 3:13-16; Mark 1:9-11; Luke 3:21,22; John 1:29-34	Paul's own experience
Matthew 28:19,20; Mark 16:15,16	Christ's example
Acts 2:38,41	Philip and Ethiopian
Acts 8:9,12,13	Paul and Philippian jailer
Acts 8:36-39	Christ's command
Acts 9:18; 22:12-16	Peter and Cornelius
Acts 10:24,47,48	Paul at Ephesus
Acts 16:14,15	3,000 saved at Pentecost
Acts 16:29-33	Paul at Corinth
Acts 18:8-11; 1 Corinthians 1:13-16	Philip in Samaria
Acts 19:1-5	Paul and Lydia

Identifying With Christ

Baptism shows that the believer is identified with Christ in His:

crucifixion

death

burial

resurrection

in order to:

walk in newness of life

G-R-A-C-E

Create an acrostic for the word *grace*. Find a word or phrase which describes or defines *grace* which begins with each of the five letters of the word. If you think of more than one word for each letter, record them all. An example of another acrostic is below.

L   Limitless
O   Open-minded
V   Valued
E   Eternal

G _____   _____

R _____

A _____   _____

C _____   _____

E _____   _____

4A - acRostic

G - goodwill · goodness · generosity
R - refinement · respect · reprieve
A - adorn - acceptance - accord · array
C - charm - courteous - compassion
E - exemption - elegance · enrich

How To Be A Victorious Christian

1. Be totally committed to Christ.

2. Believe in Christ's victory over sin and Satan.

3. Trust the grace of God.

4. Exercise self-discipline and seek to be holy.

The Holy Spirit

Psalm 51:11 . . . .

Isaiah 63:10-14 . . . .

Joel 2:28-32 . . . .

Luke 24:49 . . . .

John 14:15-17,26 . . . . . .

John 15:26 . . . .

John 16:7,13,14 . . . .

Acts 1:4,5,8 . . . .

Acts 2:1-4,38,39 . . . .

Acts 8:15-18 . . . .

Acts 9:17 . . . .

Acts 10:44-47 . . . .

Acts 19:1-6 . . . .

Who Can Be Baptized in the Holy Spirit ?

Acts 2:39 (KJV)

For the promise is unto you,

> *Peter's Jewish audience*

and to your children,

> *The next generation*

and to all that are afar off,

> *The Gentiles*

even as many as the Lord our God shall call.

> *Believers throughout history since that time*

Teamwork!

After making copies of this work sheet, cut out the numbered tasks so that each is on a separate piece of paper. Also cut off the directions and answer section at the bottom and hold on to it in case a group has a question on those items.

----

1. Sales Pitch

Select a slip of paper from the group leader and make a sales pitch for the item you have selected without actually identifying the object. The rest of the group must identify the item being promoted before your group can go on to the next task.

----

2. Mathematic Problem

Solve this problem:

A plane leaves city A and travels at 540 miles per hour toward city B. Another plane leaves city B at the same time and flies toward city A at 420 miles per hour. Cities A and B are 2,112 miles apart. How many hours will pass before the planes cross paths?

----

3. A Physical Activity

Have someone complete 10 push-ups (men's or women's, depending on the gender of the participant).

----

4. A History Question

In what year did World War II end?

----

5. A Drawing (which the rest of the small group must identify)

Select a slip of paper from the group leader and draw the item or activity identified on the slip of paper. The rest of the group must identify the item you've drawn. Your time limit is whatever time is left of the 10 minutes for all 5 of the activities.

Directions: Read to the groups the titles of the five tasks described above. Have each group decide which individual or individuals would be the best choice to attempt each task for their small group. Have them complete the tasks, one at a time, starting with the "Sales Pitch." As each group completes an activity, give them the piece of paper with the next task. Let them know they will have 10 minutes to complete all 5 activities.

Leader information—THIS IS NOT A CONTEST. Tell group members to just have fun! This is just to illustrate the different ways in which people are gifted and how the variety benefits the group.

Answers:

2. 2.2 hours or 2 hours and 12 minutes

  Formula: Time x Speed=Distance

$$T(540+420)=2,112$$
$$T=2,112 \div 960$$

4. 1945

The Gifts

Power To Know Supernaturally

The Word Of Wisdom

The Word Of Knowledge

The Distinguishing Between Spirits

Power To Act Supernaturally

Faith

Gifts Of Healing

Working of Miracles

Power To Speak Supernaturally

Prophecy

Tongues

Interpretation Of Tongues

Why We Get Sick

1. Inherent weaknesses in our human bodies (Genesis 3:19)

2. May be used by God to work out some purpose in our lives (Romans 8:28,29)

3. May make us more sympathetic toward the needs of others (2 Corinthians 1:4,6)

4. To discipline wayward believers (Numbers 12:10)

5. To serve as a judgment for sin (2 Chronicles 21:18,19)

6. To illustrate God's overall purposes (Job 2:6,7)

Case Study

Directions: Read the case study below and answer the questions that follow it. Be prepared to share your group's conclusions with the larger group.

Mr. Joseph was faithful to his church for many years. But when the church got a new pastor, he began to find other things to do on Sundays. Soon his whole family stopped going to church. When he developed a chronic illness, Mr. Joseph called for the pastor. "If God heals me, I'll come back to church," he vowed.

1. What is wrong with Mr. Joseph's promise?

2. What would you tell Mr. Joseph if he asked you to pray for him?

3. What should be the church's attitude toward him?

What Is The Lord's Supper?

1. It is a time to remember.

✝ Jesus' substitutionary death

✝ what our end would have been had we not accepted Jesus as Savior

2. It is a time to anticipate Christ's return.

3. It is a time to evaluate our attitude.

4. It is a time to fellowship.

✝ Christian with Christian

✝ Christian with Christ

Resource 8A, *Biblical Foundations*. Permission to mechanically reproduce this resource granted for local church use.
©1997 Gospel Publishing House

There's A Place For All

Cast: Moderator

Brother Eye

Sister Hand

Brother Little Toe

Props: This is up to your group. It might be good to at least wear name cards.

Moderator: Brother Eye has a problem with Sister Hand.

Eye: (*strutting around*) Everyone knows how important I am. The hands would be practically useless without the eyes to guide them.

Hand: Nonsense! (*with attitude*) This body doesn't operate by sight alone. Feeling is important too, you know.

Eye: Oh, yeah? (*tauntingly*) Why did Jesus say, "Don't let your left hand know what your right hand is doing?" Didn't He also say to cut off your hand if it causes you to sin?

Hand: (*sarcastically*) Of course He said that. (*Look at the rest of the group and pause.*) Right after He said to pluck out your eye if it causes you to sin. (*laughs*) The body needs a hand to pluck out its eye.

Moderator: (*breaking in*) It looks like we will have to let a third party judge between you two.

Hand: OK by me. I'm sure I will be given the victory.

Eye: (*interrupting*) Not so fast! I'm sure it will be obvious how important I am.

Moderator: (*in grand style*) May I present the judge, Brother Little Toe.

Eye and Hand: (*in unison, with disbelief*) Brother Little Toe?

(*Little Toe should start out standing tall—confident, not proud—then begin to question his own usefulness and act unsure.*)

Eye: What does he know about seeing?

Hand: And what does he know about handling objects? All he's good for is getting bumped on the-coffee table.

Eye and Hand: (*in unison again*) We protest!

Moderator: May I remind you both of 1 Corinthians 6:4? (*Have Bible open to text and read.*) Brother Little Toe will settle the argument. Both of you will abide by his decision. (*Brother Little Toe stands tall again.*) And that's final

BIBLICAL FOUNDATIONS, LEADER'S GUIDE

What Can I Do?

You might be amazed what you can do for your church. Below is a list of some responsibilities and ministry opportunities in a church. Read over the list and check the items which apply to you. Your church may not have need for all these ministries or may have even more from which to choose. **THIS IS NOT A SIGN-UP SHEET. IT IS ONLY A SURVEY.**

I have work experience in the following areas:

___Architectural Design
___Accounting
___Art
___Auto Mechanics
___Building Maintenance
___Bus Driver
___Camp Director
___Child Care

___Coaching
___Creative Writing
___Custodial
___Interior Design
___Lawn Care
___Librarian
___Medicine
___Music

___Printing
___Public Relations
___Publishing
___Receptionist
___Sales
___Secretarial
___Teaching
___Technical Writing

I have the following talents:

Computer Skills
___Hardware Analysis
___Software Analysis
___Program Design

Vocal
___Solo
___Choir

Other_____
_____
_____
_____
_____

Creative Arts
___Graphic Design
___Drawing
___Writing
___Drama

Instrumental
_____Instrument
___Composing
___Conducting
___Other

_____
_____
_____
_____
_____

I would be interested in serving in the following ministries:

___Bookkeeping
___Building Maintenance
___Children's Ministry
___Driver—Van/Bus
___Evangelism Team
___Greeter
___Home Cell Group Leader
___Janitorial
___Jr. High Ministry
___Lawn Care
___Men's Ministry

___Missions Outreach
___Music Ministry:
___Choir
___Musical Solo
___Orchestra
___Sound System Operator
___Nursery
___Prayer Warrior (Intercessory)
___Preaching
___Public Relations
___Receptionist

___Secretarial
___Seniors' Ministry
___Singles' Ministry
___Sunday School Teacher
age level_____
___Ushering
___Visitor Follow-Up
___Women's Ministry
___Youth Ministry
Other_____
_____

Name: _____

Address: _____

Phone: _____

Examples Of Faithful Stewardship

1. The Macedonians
(2 Corinthians 8:1-5)

2. The Poor Widow
(Luke 21:1-4)

3. Jesus
(John 17:5; 2 Corinthians 8:9;
Philippians 2:5-8)

4. Abraham
(Genesis 14:18-20)

5. Jacob
(Genesis 28:20-22)

Who Would Want To Do Less?

Jesus gave up everything He had in heaven so we could be saved from our sins. He used everything given to Him to complete His task. Stewardship involves many aspects of our lives, not just our finances. How we manage all the things we have is a reflection of our affection and respect for God. Take a few minutes to complete the work sheet below. It is designed to help you discover and evaluate the amount of time you are presently dedicating to God. It is only for your information and self-evaluation.

1. How much time in an average week do you spend in devotional Bible study?

2. How much time in an average week do you spend in devotional prayer?

3. How much time in an average week do you spend in attendance at services in your local church?

4. What percentage of your check is given in tithes *and* offerings to your local church?

5. What additional amount of time and/or money do you give to any parachurch ministries?

6. How much time in an average week do you spend in direct evangelism?

7. How much time in an average week do you spend praying for other people's salvation and needs?

8. How much time in an average week do you spend in direct service to your local church?

9. Write down anything you do, aside from a job, to which you give more time, money, or energy than you do to God and His work.

10. Based on your answers to the above questions, are you satisfied with how you are using and distributing the things God has given you?

11. How would you like to improve your usage of God's possessions?

12. What are some practical ways to reach your goal?

☞ Increase my giving to $ _____ per week

☞ Increase my devotional time to: _____ hours per week studying

_____ hours per week praying

☞ Increase my service to the local church to _____ hours per week

☞ Increase my parachurch service to _____ hours per week

☞ Increase my prayer time for other people to _____ hours per week

☞ Increase my time spent in personal evangelism to _____ hours per week

Bapa's Quest

Bapa Timmy lived in a mountain village on Buru, one of the thousands of islands that make up the Republic of Indonesia. Like all Buruese, Bapa was an animist. He worshiped his ancestors and sought to appease the evil spirits he believed inhabited such objects as rocks, trees, and man-made fetishes.

Sometime around 1942, tragedy struck Bapa's family. Ten of his brothers and sisters died. In his sorrow, Bapa turned from his animism and began to search for the unknown God he believed must exist somewhere. And God, who reaches out to every searching heart, began to reveal himself to Bapa. Realizing his fetishes were sinful, Bapa destroyed them and cried out to the God whose name he did not know, asking forgiveness for sins.

Bapa built a house where he and his family gathered whenever he felt moved to worship. During these meetings they wept in the presence of God and sang songs they composed. Bapa exhorted the others to live moral lives and forbade the use of tobacco and betel nuts—stimulants used in Indonesia. Soon up to 100 people were worshiping with Bapa.

God used various miracles to speak to Bapa and those who joined him in worship. Once, as they crowded into the meetinghouse, they all fell to the ground under the powerful presence of God.

On another occasion Bapa was called to a nearby village to pray for a sick woman. By the time he arrived, she had died. God revealed to Bapa that her son's wickedness had caused her death. When the boy repented of his sins, life returned to the woman. Because of this miracle, many people believed in Bapa's God, and a meeting place was built in the village.

During a long drought, other villagers prayed to their gods without result. Finally they asked Bapa to pray. God answered by sending rain, and many of the villagers accepted Him.

Angered because so many people were turning to Bapa's God, 30 armed warriors came down from the mountains, beat Bapa unmercifully, and left him to die. Bapa survived, but within a week, most of the warriors were dead. The remaining six were afflicted with various ailments they believed were punishment for their attack. They went to Bapa, accepted his God, and were healed.

In a song Bapa composed, he mentioned Jesus. Although he did not know the meaning of this name, his heart had been stirred when he heard it on a trip to the coast.

In 1952 Bapa met Johan Hukum, an Assemblies of God man. As Johan explained God's plan of salvation, Bapa recognized this was the truth to which God had been leading him for the past 10 years.

God continued to use miracles in confirming Bapa Timmy's witness. Once, when 77 unbelievers rose up against Bapa, he prophesied a tree would fall on each of their houses. When this prophecy came to pass, all these animists turned to the Lord and brought their fetishes to Bapa. A fire was built, and a box filled with the fetishes was laid on the flames. Through the demon power the fetishes contained, the box jumped from the fire. Pleading the blood of Jesus, Bapa put the box back on the fire and held it down with a stick. The fetishes were finally destroyed.

On another occasion, Bapa Timmy experienced a miracle similar to that of Elijah and the prophets of Baal. Buru had suffered a 9-month drought. The local witch doctors challenged Bapa Timmy to a contest to see whose god would produce rain. They gathered on a large, open area on a hillside. All around the ground was parched and burned by a recent forest fire.

The witch doctors prayed to their gods, but the drought continued. Then Bapa Timmy took his turn. He said he would pray for 1 week, and then the rain would come. He named the exact time it would rain. The following week, Bapa Timmy and the witch doctors gathered again. The sky was clear. Then, at the time Bapa Timmy had predicted, rain began to pour down all around, but the spot were the men stood remained dry.

Bapa Timmy died in 1988 at 91, but his spiritual legacy lives on in at least 13 churches that were planted through his ministry. Bapa's quest for the true God has led many to the Truth.

Source: Whosoever!, a Division of Foreign Missions publication, Assemblies of God, 1991.

The Partnership Of Missions

I was doing everything I knew to do, but I couldn't raise the support to get my family to the mission field of our calling. Was that really what God wanted us to do? Did we miss the will of God? Many times I recalled our interview with personnel in the Division of Foreign Missions. They did challenge my ability to raise support. They even asked if I thought my speech impediment would hurt my public speaking. (I didn't know I had a problem until then. Been worried about it ever since.)

I hadn't pastored and hadn't preached much. I was entering a missions career out of a journalism background.

After one of my first itineration services a man came up to me and said, "Brother Barefield, you remind me of my brother."

"I do?" I asked.

"Yeah," he replied. "He's trying to be a preacher too. I think he knows what he wants to say, but he can't say it either."

My pat answer to the Division of Foreign Missions back then had been, "God called me. I have no doubt in *His* ability to raise our budget."

That was theory. Reality was settling in.

I was ready to quit missions. (I mean *really* quit—an itinerating missionary has many passing thoughts of quitting.) I went to a friend, and we prayed in his home. After that I had an assurance that God was at work in our lives.

The next week I got a phone call from a widow. About a year earlier, a gift she had intended for another missionary account was placed in ours by mistake. We forwarded the gift to the right account, but she ended up on our mailing list.

The gist of the call: She knew of our need by my newsletters. God had spoken to her, and she had called to tell me to take my family to the field—she would make up the difference in my budget. She asked how much we needed. I told her we were short $1,250 per month.

"You go, and I'll send in the support," she said.

"Wait a minute, Sister Emma. I need $1,250 every month, not just one time."

"I know," she answered. "Send me a pledge form, and I'll sign it."

We went to the field. Every month our account received a check for $1,250 from a lady we had never met. We still haven't met her.

She provided the thrust to get us to the field. If Sister Emma had not listened to God and responded, our missionary career would have been over.

Missionaries have responded to the call. They are willing to leave family, friends, and careers to plant His Church on foreign soil. However, they must have supporters like Sister Emma.

I have since learned that at that time Sister Emma's was the largest personal pledge on record. Not everyone can make a $1,250 monthly pledge. Some will give $12.50 or $25 or $50. Or a one-time gift.

By the way, I'm not sure I ever did have a speech impediment, but I did stutter the day Sister Emma called.

Reprinted from the *Pentecostal Evangel*, November 10, 1996, "Sister Emma," by Ron Barefield.

Step-By-Step

Amish Friendship Bread—the name says it all: it is a bread of friendship, designed to be shared. The instructions for making this bread don't end with its original recipe. Read through the recipe and instructions for the original starter. Following are instructions for your friends with whom you share starters. As you will see, these starters have specific steps to be followed as well and should then be split and shared. Once initiated, Amish Friendship Bread can be shared perpetually without ever having to be started from scratch again. The important thing to remember is each step must be taken in order—one cannot be skipped, nor can one be rushed. The recipe is a success only when followed a step at a time.

Making the original starter:

1 cup flour, all-purpose	1/2 cup sugar
1 cup warm water	1 tablespoon yeast

Mix all ingredients in a glass bowl, using a wooden spoon. Cover loosely with lid or plate. Let stand in a warm place. Stir each day. On the 5th and 10th days add 1 cup flour, 1 cup milk, and 1 cup sugar.

After adding the ingredients on the 10th day, separate the mixture into 1-cup starters. Keep 1 cup for yourself and pass on the others (2 or 3 cups) to friends. To your cup combine: 1 cup oil, 1/2 cup milk, 3 eggs, and 1 tsp. vanilla.

In a separate bowl, mix:

2 cups flour	1 tsp. salt	1 cup sugar
1 1/2 tsp. baking powder	1 large box instant vanilla pudding	2 tsp. cinnamon
1/2 tsp. baking soda	1 cup chopped nuts (optional)	

Add dry ingredients to wet mixture and mix thoroughly. Pour into two well-greased 2-quart loaf pans that have been coated with a cinnamon and sugar mixture. Sprinkle extra cinnamon and sugar on top. **Bake at 325° for 1 hour.**

Working with a shared starter: (Share the info below with the friends to whom you give the starters.)

USE LARGE (ONE GALLON) ZIPLOC-TYPE BAGS * DO NOT REFRIGERATE * DO NOT USE METAL SPOON

Day 1 -	Do nothing.
Days 2,3,4,5 -	Mash (squeeze) ingredients in bag. (Do not open bag.)
Day 6 -	Add to bag 1 cup each: flour, sugar, milk. Mash ingredients together in bag.
Days 7,8,9 -	Mash ingredients in bag. Let air out afterwards.
Day 10 -	Add to bag 1 cup each: sugar, milk. Stir with wooden spoon.

Pour 1-cup starters into large Ziploc-type bags and share with friends (should have 3 or 4 cups to share).

Pour last cup into a large bowl and combine with: 1 cup oil, 1/2 cup milk, 3 eggs, and 1 tsp. vanilla.

In a separate bowl, mix:

2 cups flour	1 tsp. salt	1 cup sugar
1 1/2 tsp. baking powder	1 large box instant vanilla pudding	2 tsp. cinnamon
1/2 tsp. baking soda	1 cup chopped nuts (optional)	

Add dry ingredients to wet mixture and mix thoroughly. Pour into two well-greased 2-quart loaf pans that have been coated with a cinnamon and sugar mixture. Sprinkle extra cinnamon and sugar on top. **Bake at 325° for 1 hour.**

Know The Scripture

Listed below are Scripture passages which help explain to someone the need, promise, and plan of salvation. The more familiar we are with Scripture (location, meaning, etc.) the better witnesses we will be. Our understanding of Scripture needs to be broader than these passages though. We need to be prepared to answer other questions an individual might have. Remember, the Holy Spirit will bring things to our memory when we need it. Try to memorize one or two of these passages a week until you have all of them memorized. Write the passages on index cards and carry them with you. Test yourself every week or so on all you have memorized so the first passages aren't forgotten as new ones are added.

Genesis 12:1-3	Matthew 1:21
Exodus 12:29-42	Luke 1:76-79
Deuteronomy 26:6-9	Luke 19:10
1 Samuel 2:1,2	John 1:12
Psalm 13:5,6	John 3:14-17
Psalm 18:1-3	John 11:25,26
Psalm 27:1	John 20:31
Psalm 37:39,40	Acts 4:12
Psalm 62:1-8	Acts 13:38,39
Psalm 85:4-7	Romans 1:16
Psalm 98:1-3	Romans 3:21-26
Psalm 116:1-13	Romans 10:4-13
Isaiah 12:1-3	1 Corinthians 15:1-8
Isaiah 25:9	2 Corinthians 5:17 to 6:1
Isaiah 43:11-13	Galatians 2:16
Isaiah 51:4-6	Ephesians 2:4-9
Isaiah 53:6-12	1 Thessalonians 5:8-10
Isaiah 55:6,7	2 Thessalonians 2:13
Isaiah 59:15-17	1 Timothy 1:15,16
Isaiah 61:10	1 Timothy 2:3-6
Isaiah 63:1-6	2 Timothy 3:15
Jeremiah 23:5,6	Titus 3:3-7
Ezekiel 3:16-21	Hebrews 2:3
Ezekiel 18:21-23	Hebrews 5:9
Ezekiel 33:14-16	Hebrews 7:25
Joel 2:32	1 John 5:11,12
Micah 7:7	Revelation 3:20

Various Views Of The Rapture

Most evangelical Christians embrace a premillennial view of the rapture of the Church. This means that Christ will gather His saints before establishing His 1000-year reign on earth. There are various views, however, concerning when the actual event will take place. Following are the three most commonly held views by those who believe in a pre-millennial rapture of the Church.

Pre-Tribulation Rapture

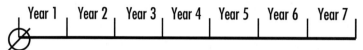

The pre-Tribulation view of the rapture of the Church states that Jesus will come for those who are "ready and waiting" His return. Christians will be caught up together and will celebrate the Marriage Supper of the Lamb. This catching away of the bride of Christ precedes the 7 years of tribulation. The raptured Christians will accompany Jesus when He returns to do battle with Satan at the end of the Tribulation. Those who hold a pre-Tribulation position believe Christians will escape the wrath of God, which will occur during the Great Tribulation, and establish Jesus' millennial kingdom.

Mid-Tribulation Rapture

The mid-Tribulation view of the rapture of the Church states that Christians will be present during the first 42 months of the great Tribulation. During that time they will be protected from the disasters that confront unredeemed humanity. At the end of the first 42 months (or halfway through the Tribulation) those who have accepted Jesus as Lord and Savior will be caught up to meet Jesus in the sky. The saints will celebrate the Marriage Supper of the Lamb. The raptured Christians will accompany Jesus when He returns to do battle with Satan at the end of the Tribulation and establish Jesus' millennial kingdom.

Post-Tribulation Rapture

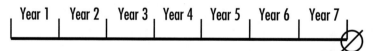

The post-Tribulation view of the rapture of the Church states that Christians will be present during the entire 7-year Tribulation. They will avoid God's wrath which is directed at the unsaved, much as the Israelites were spared in the land of Goshen (Exodus 8:22,23). Christians will have to endure persecution dealt by the Antichrist, looking to God for strength and comfort. At the conclusion of the Great Tribulation, the saved will meet Jesus in the air, change in the "twinkling of an eye," and immediately return with Jesus to do battle with Satan and establish Jesus' millennial kingdom.

VIEWS OF THE MILLENNIUM

AMILLENNIALIST:

❏ No literal Millennium on earth

❏ Book of Revelation is symbolic

❏ General resurrection after the Church Age, then new heaven and new earth

❏ No restoration of Israel, all prophecies applied to the Church

❏ Augustine of Hippo, chief proponent

POSTMILLENNIALIST:

❏ Millennium is extension of the Church Age

❏ Whole world will be won to Christ, then a general resurrection and the new heaven and new earth

❏ No restoration of the nation of Israel

❏ No literal reign of Christ on earth

❏ Kingdom of God will not be brought in through judgment

PREMILLENNIALIST:

❏ Interpret prophecies of O.T. and N.T. as literally as possible

❏ A literal 1,000-year reign of Christ on earth

❏ Millennium comes after the Rapture, the Great Tribulation, Judgment Seat of Christ, and the Revelation of Christ

❏ Literal restoration of the nation of Israel

❏ Position accepted by most evangelical churches

PANORAMA OF PROPHECY

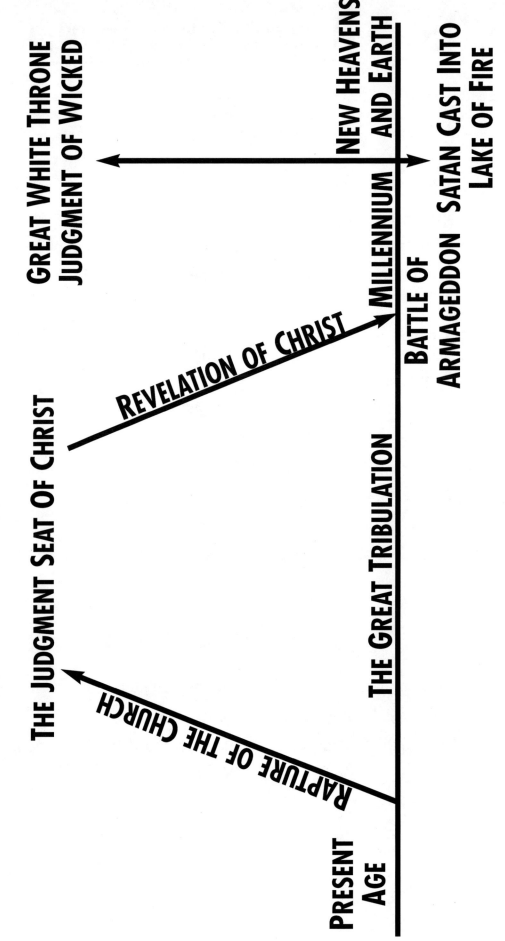

THE MARRIAGE SUPPER OF THE LAMB

GREAT WHITE THRONE JUDGMENT OF WICKED

THE JUDGMENT SEAT OF CHRIST

REVELATION OF CHRIST

NEW HEAVENS AND EARTH

SATAN CAST INTO LAKE OF FIRE

MILLENNIUM

BATTLE OF ARMAGEDDON

THE GREAT TRIBULATION

RAPTURE OF THE CHURCH

PRESENT AGE

BIBLICAL FOUNDATIONS, LEADER'S GUIDE

Biblical Foundations Evaluation

Please complete this form and return it to the publisher. We are interested in your opinion of our curricular material. We will use your insights and suggestions as we develop additional titles in the *Spiritual Discovery Series*. We would be interested in hearing from you whether you have positive comments or negative. The editorial staff of the *Spiritual Discovery Series* wish to develop a product that ministers to the needs of our users. Thank you in advance for taking a few moments to complete this evaluation.

1. In what study setting was the title *Biblical Foundations* used?

_____ Individual   _____ Home Fellowship   _____ Sunday School   _____ Other: _____

2. What was your initial reaction to the following?

	Excellent	Good	Poor
Cover Art	_____	_____	_____
Appearance Of Inside Text	_____	_____	_____
Size Of The Leader's Guide	_____	_____	_____
Size Of The Study Guide	_____	_____	_____
Spiral Binding	_____	_____	_____
Price Of Leader's Guide	_____	_____	_____

3. How do you evaluate the usefulness of the following?

	Excellent	Good	Poor
Spiral Binding	_____	_____	_____
Leader's Methodology	_____	_____	_____
Resource Pages	_____	_____	_____
Study Guide Text In Leader's Guide	_____	_____	_____

4. How effective were the following elements of the curriculum?

	Excellent	Good	Poor
Study Objectives	_____	_____	_____
Getting The Group's Attention	_____	_____	_____
Transition Statements	_____	_____	_____
Methodology	_____	_____	_____
Let's Review	_____	_____	_____
Resource Pages	_____	_____	_____
Study Guide Material	_____	_____	_____

5. On a scale of 1 to 5 (5 being excellent), how do you rate the "user friendliness" of the product? _____

6. Did most group members complete the study guide material before they arrived at the session? _____

7. Did group members actively participate in group sessions? _____

8. What was the most useful element of the product?

9. How would you improve the product to make it more useful for the leader?

10. Additional Comments:

_____
_____
_____

Biblical Foundations

Place
Stamp
Here

SPIRITUAL DISCOVERY SERIES
1445 N. BOONVILLE AVENUE
SPRINGFIELD MO   65802-1894